MINDING THE FUTURE

Revitalizing Learning Cultures Through Teacher Leadership

ANGELINE A. ANDERSON
SUSAN K. BORG
STEPHANIE L. EDGAR

A Joint Publication

A SAGE Publishing Company

FOR INFORMATION:

Corwin

A SAGE Company

2455 Teller Road

Thousand Oaks, California 91320

(800) 233-9936

www.corwin.com

SAGE Publications Ltd.

1 Oliver's Yard

55 City Road

London EC1Y 1SP

United Kingdom

SAGE Publications India Pvt. Ltd.

B 1/I 1 Mohan Cooperative Industrial Area

Mathura Road, New Delhi 110 044

India

SAGE Publications Asia-Pacific Pte. Ltd.

3 Church Street

#10-04 Samsung Hub

Singapore 049483

Publisher: Arnis Burvikovs

Development Editor: Desirée Bartlett

Editorial Assistant: Eliza Erickson

Production Editor: Amy Schroller

Copy Editor: Diana Breti

Typesetter: C&M Digitals (P) Ltd.

Proofreader: Dennis W. Webb

Indexer: Sheila Bodell

Cover Designer: Gail Buschman

Marketing Manager: Maura Sullivan

Printed in the United States of America

ISBN 978-1-5443-1828-8

This book is printed on acid-free paper.

SUSTAINABLE FORESTRY INITIATIVE

Certified Chain of Custody

Promoting Sustainable Forestry

www.sfiprogram.org

SFI-01268

SFI label applies to text stock

18 19 20 21 22 10 9 8 7 6 5 4 3 2 1

Contents

CHAPTER 2. Developing Collaborative Innovators: Session 1   22

Visit resources.corwin.com/MindingTheFuture
for downloadable resources.

MINDING THE FUTURE

To all teachers who inspire, innovate, and transform the future.

Online Resources

Introduction

Chapter 1

Chapter 2

Chapter 3

Chapter 4

Visit resources.corwin.com/MindingTheFuture
for downloadable resources.

Preface

I have learned that I would rather flirt with failure than never dance with my joy.

—WES MOORE

Professional Learning to Inspire Vision and Voice

Imagine a school district conference room on a warm day in early June filled with enthusiastic educators excited about *teaching, learning,* and *risk-taking change!* No one is complaining about state testing, thinks that the coming break will be too short, or dreads another summer of training. Now consider that these educators have just completed a year-long series of monthly professional learning days centered on *possibilities, community, and innovative learning practices.* All of this in the age of assessment and accountability.

It *is* possible to find a smiling, laughing, inspired roomful of teachers and principals eager to share their accomplishments, failures, and transformations even at the end of a long school year. It is not a dream that professional learning can transform stressed school employees who used to say, "Just tell me what to do," into innovative, collaborative instructional professionals who gladly suggest strategies, websites, books, devices, furniture, and even wall paint colors to colleagues.

This book tells the story of a journey that started with some enticing questions:

- What does it mean for today's students to be future ready and what will it take to get them there?
- What will prepare our teachers and principals to be ready to lead this change or will they be left behind or replaced?

- What is the future of education when technology is changing so quickly?

- What kind of learner is needed to meet the needs of our communities and the world?

- What are the best tools and learning environments available to meet the challenge of *minding the future*?

With so many questions, it becomes apparent that no one resource, researcher, or person could supply all the answers. Solutions are available, however, in one undeniable place: the practitioners already in schools who are struggling to meet the future in districts that function by systematically fulfilling state and federal regulations. They need a new type of professional learning, one that moves beyond standardization to innovation and encourages collaborative support for transformative change rather than sustains isolated islands of novel performance. This professional learning honors creative thinking, induces risk taking, and explores the world students will enter outside the classroom. This journey cannot be without bumps in the road, questions, nay-sayers, or worry. It takes encouragement to let go of the way things have always been done and hard work on the part of the participants to explore new ways of thinking and doing. In the end, you will find that change is possible, risk taking is learning, and skilled practitioners really do make the difference. We called this experience the Transform Academy, where committed teachers learn the skills to grow into teacher leaders who are empowered to revitalize the learning cultures in their schools. These teacher leaders, and the principals who support them, are minding the future for our students.

Embarking on an educational change process driven by teacher voice requires a starting point from which the participants have common understandings in pedagogy, collaboration, and planning. First, a well-defined understanding of instructional best practices including curriculum expectations, student assessment techniques, and intervention/enrichment strategies aids participants in defining expectations and the work of the classroom. Second, experience working in professional learning communities improves communication and provides a framework for discussions and proposing ideas. Finally, data-driven goal setting and action plans provide evidence that support or refute the implementation of new ideas. These concepts are considered to be a foundation so that principals and teachers alike may participate fully in the change process while continuing to meet current regulations, standards, and community needs.

Audience

This book is for those who ask, "Is the way we have always done school the only way?" It is for those who see learning as the stuff of inspiration and growth and whose vision and voice are quietly demonstrated in classrooms across the globe daily. It speaks to those who see no limits in their service to others and who embrace tomorrow's potential and the positive opportunities that come with knowing that they truly do touch the future. Throughout these pages we welcome teachers, principals, central office administrators, and professional learning staff to engage in conversations about the future of education and its potential to meet learners where they are and guide them to pursue their dreams. Using vision, collaboration, and research to lead the way, we ask readers to reconsider our current industrial model of teaching and instead embrace the collective power of an inspired professional team of teachers who can, through their innovative feats, transform the way students grow and learn.

Transform Academy Design

Our professional learning and curriculum departments planned and facilitated the academy to encourage and promote the kind of teacher voice that inspires innovations in instructional environments and practices. Each academy involved approximately 10 campuses, with three teachers from each campus coming together to participate in a full day of learning once a month for nine months. That's 30 teachers working together as a team for approximately 72 hours per academic year. Principals served as sounding boards and guides as teachers explored and tried out innovative instructional approaches. When you implement a professional learning academy in your own school or district, you may have more or fewer teacher-participants, but we encourage you to select a core group of teachers who are willing to commit to the initiative for a full year, meet regularly, and gladly share their growth and obstacles with one another throughout the year in both formal and informal ways. As school leaders, principals interested in this kind of transformative change should endeavor to fully support the academy teachers by communicating regularly through calendared collaborative meetings and informal conversations as needed.

Who We Are

Throughout this book you will see us describe *what* we did, *why* we used certain research-based approaches, and *how* we planned, along with the insights we discovered. "We," the three authors of this book, along with members of the curriculum and professional learning teams, were involved in the planning and implementation, day-to-day facilitation, and debriefing of our district Transform Academies. We wrote this book to share the insights we gained from this experience and as a step-by-step guide so that you, too, can implement year-long, teacher-led professional learning academies in your own schools and districts. Our intention is to give enough guidance to be clear and to facilitate easy replication but to also leave plenty of room for you to tailor your own academies to meet your needs. By outlining our process, we hope that you, too, will be able to revitalize the learning cultures in your school by empowering skilled teacher leaders who will mind the future of your students.

Organization of This Book

We begin each chapter with stories and thoughts about what we learned from our teachers, principals, and students. These stories combine the voices and ideas of several people into one person and are not written to represent any specific individual. We have intentionally not used the names of our academy participants to protect their privacy. After the stories, some related research and theories are given to support these findings and explain why we employed these ideas. Discussion questions, session activity descriptions, and possible action items conclude each chapter. Each set of questions and activities is created to encourage professional growth, create a risk-free environment, and guide readers in how each academy session promotes and embraces innovation and transformation!

Following this preface, the Introduction to the Transform Academy provides a project preview. Next, Chapter 1 furnishes readers with guidance for the pre-session work. This work aids a team in determining the readiness of a learning culture to transform. This chapter also provides readers with ways to use this book for differentiated leadership planning. In Chapters 2 to 7, readers are afforded the *what*, *why*, and *how* of the nine academy sessions. Throughout these pages, we focus on the importance of future-ready visioning to overcome educational status quo thinking and encourage professional learning communities to grow as collaborative innovators. To do this, we explore strategies that empower teachers to dream, research, and find their collective voices while creating flexible learning environments. This leads to a look at the dynamics of student-led learning and then to methods to sustain the positive momentum built by teacher-led professional learning. Chapter 8 closes this book with our parting thoughts. As you read, we hope you will find ways to employ these ideas and learn from our experiences. Further, we would love to hear from you as you make the Transform Academy journey!

Acknowledgments

If we truly wish to mind the future, we must seek and appreciate the brilliance of others.

—ANGELINE A. ANDERSON, SUSAN K. BORG, STEPHANIE L. EDGAR

Over our educational careers, we have learned that empowering learners means having a mindset that states, "Given opportunity, knowledge and a collaborative network, individuals will excel beyond expectations." As we asked teachers and principals to "mind the future," this thinking gave us the resolve to quietly guide and carefully listen while they did the real work of leading their learning cultures through instructional transformation. Alongside them, intrepid students supplied creative ideas and feedback regarding classroom changes. We would like to thank all of the Transform Academy participants for their vision and eagerness to design engaging learning experiences while revitalizing the ways we think about schools.

While writing this book, we found many of the same mindset attributes are needed to produce a manuscript for publication. In the spirit of collaboration, we sought assistance from some exceptional people. We offer our deep appreciation to Craig Hampton, who led us through the doors of Corwin and introduced us to Arnis Burvikovs, Desirée Bartlett, and Eliza Erickson. We thank each of you for your gracious guidance. Jackie Walsh and Beth Sattes, authors of *Thinking Through Quality Questioning*, kindly advised and cheered us along the way. We owe them our sincere gratitude.

We also wish to thank our superintendent, support staff, and facilitation teams for believing in and promoting the Transform Academy. Your patience as innovations emerged, meeting agendas changed, new technologies entered the network, and oddly shaped furniture arrived at the warehouse is appreciated.

To our families, we say thank you a million times for giving us the time and encouragement needed to gather our thoughts and put them into words. Without the wisdom and strength of our parents—Geneva Wessel, Gerald Procknow, and Margaretta Anderson—this book would not have been possible. Finally, heartfelt love and gratitude goes to our courageous husbands, Russ Edgar, Dean Borg, and Larry Schkade—great listeners and founts of support!

Publisher's Acknowledgments

Corwin gratefully acknowledges the contributions of the following reviewers:

Rich Hall
Director of Elementary Education
Henrico, VA

Jacie Maslyk
Assistant Superintendent
Coraopolis, PA

Jessica McMillan
Instructional Coach
Pensacola, FL

Laura Von Staden
ESE Lead Teacher
Tampa, FL

About the Authors

Angeline A. Anderson, PhD, is currently an independent educational consultant. She is formerly the executive director for instruction in a large suburban school district in Texas, where she oversaw the activities of 124 staff members whose mission was to provide high-quality curriculum, assessments, media services, and professional development to district teachers and staff. Her experience as an educator includes classroom teacher, counselor, administrator, program evaluator, statistician, and district leader. Dr. Anderson has served students and teachers in Florida, Texas, and California. Her work and interests include social cognitive theory, quality schools, strategic planning, curriculum development, instructional technology, response to intervention, and leadership. She has presented at state and national conferences on a variety of strategies to transform instructional processes using technology integration.

Susan K. Borg, EdD, is a clinical assistant professor at Sam Houston State University where she supervises the superintendent certification program and teaches graduate-level principal preparation courses, as well as a senior associate at N2 Learning, an educational consulting company. She is formerly the associate superintendent for instruction and student services and was the supervisor of the academic programs for approximately 50,000 students in a suburban school district in Texas. Dr. Borg facilitated the collaboration of six instructional and data accountability departments at the district level with 44 campuses, prekindergarten through Grade 12. Prior to becoming associate superintendent, Dr. Borg served the field of education for 34 years as a teacher, assistant principal, principal, and executive director. She has presented at state and national conferences on the importance of the integration of innovation and technology into instructional processes for the educational preparation of future-ready students.

Stephanie L. Edgar, MEd, is currently an associate at N2 Learning, an educational consulting company, and teaches in the Department of Curriculum and Instruction at the University of Houston, supporting students in the teacher education program. She is formerly the director of campus instructional support in a large suburban school district in Texas. Her team provided direct support to campuses through professional development, specialist training, video production, adaptive and benchmark assessments, campus planning, and embedded technology. Mrs. Edgar has provided in-depth training in the areas of planning, professional learning communities, assessments for learning, collaborative consultations, critical conversations, instructional best practices, student and teacher portfolios, and online professional development. She has served students and teachers for 38 years as a teacher, instructional specialist, and district administrator. Her presentations at state and national conferences focus on leading innovative professional learning, student engagement, and opportunities for transformative teacher leadership.

Introduction to the Transform Academy

The electric light did not come from the continuous improvement of candles.

—OREN HARARI

Scope, Purpose, and Goals

Simply stated, the Transform Academy is a facilitated professional "Think Tank" in which teachers meet once a month for a year to study and implement innovative instructional best practices as a Professional Learning Community (PLC). During this year, teachers are asked to implement their new learning by following a Personal Learning Plan (PLP), which they develop with a team or individually. Their projects are then showcased at a Learning Fair at the end of the year. Although an academy may be led by principals or lead teachers at a campus, the work we describe in this book was led by a district-level learning design team whose expertise included professional learning, curriculum development, language acquisition, special populations, technology integration, and whole-child education. Our participants represented staff from our early childhood to high school campuses. Using our ideas, the composition of your lead team or academy may be different but still very successful. The scale of your academy may be as small as a pilot of a few teachers working at a single campus or as large as our cross-sectional district group composed of 30 or more participants. We encourage you to consider your needs as you read our experiences and suggestions in the pages that follow.

The purpose of an academy differs from the still necessary but typical professional learning found in most districts or conference formats. This model is an extension of the foundational instructional elements teachers already possess. These elements include knowledge of instructional best practices in curriculum, assessment, intervention, and enrichment. Further, this model is based on a teacher's commitment to working collaboratively with other teachers and his or her willingness to utilize data and planning for the benefit of students. Thus, the purpose of a Transform Academy is unlike other professional learning opportunities and is founded in the use of a variety of strategies and research techniques to spark teacher imagination, resulting in innovative learning methods and environments. This new learning is, in turn, available for other teachers to consider and utilize. The overarching goal of a Transform Academy is to open the doors of a teacher's imagination and to develop and support an empowered group of thought leaders willing to implement innovations resulting in research-based, transformed, student-centered learning environments. These are the leaders who will propel their campuses, districts, and communities beyond standards and accountability and into the future.

Transform Academy Design: Informing Our Driving Vision

A project of this magnitude requires a well-crafted roadmap. In addition to adding the academy to the district strategic plan, we used a project-based learning model for planning the academy. Figure I.1 provides a sample of our design.

The **driving question,** like a problem statement, links the academy's goals and purpose to intended products and outcomes: *What does it mean when we say we want our students to be future ready?* This question presents teachers with an authentic challenge, giving them a chance to address their current realities and concerns with like-minded colleagues. It also requires consideration of what the future will be like for students as they progress through school and into the workplace. What does minding the future entail? **Learning outcomes** or **transformation targets** specifically identify key knowledge and understanding, such as *communication, collaboration, critical thinking, and creativity.* These 21st-century skills, along with technology usage, were intentionally utilized throughout the activities for each session. **Checkpoints** were embedded in the activities throughout the sessions to assess the effectiveness of the plan and to make adjustments as necessary. Honest feedback from the teachers allowed us to make the changes resulting in sessions personalized for their needs. These checkpoints also provided opportunities for us to **formatively assess** teacher acquisition of the key knowledge and understanding

Figure I.1 Sample Project-Based Learning Design: Transform Academy

Project Design: Sparking Innovation and Transformation
Project: Transform Academy
Driving Question: What does it mean when we say we want our students to be *future ready*?

Innovative Products	Learning Outcomes/ Transformation Targets	Checkpoints/ Formative Assessments	Instructional Strategies for Professional Learning
• Learning Fair • Provide required technology training sessions at respective campuses • Presentation to school board and community members	• Application of 21st-century skills in the Transform Academy sessions and in the classroom • Demonstrate ability to use various technology apps	• Personal learning plan developed with leading and lagging indicators (PLP) • Timeline monitored throughout the year • Written reflections • Mini-surveys	• Study of research articles and professional texts • Technology training • Field trips • Consultants • Furniture showcase

of the 21st-century skills identified in the project design. During the checkpoints, participant feedback was also gathered using surveys, written reflections, and PLP progress checks. Learning Fair presentations provided both the participants and facilitators with important summative information regarding successful innovations and ways to sustain this learning and then move it forward.

Participant Selection

Our campus principals selected the participants for our academies using an application process. We informed principals about the purpose and overall goals of the academy and provided the Agreement to Participate in the Transform Academy forms found in Online Resource A. A synopsis of the qualifications, requirements, and responsibilities found on the agreement form are listed below. The online form offers more detail and can easily be modified to fit the needs, expectations, and policies of your school community.

Qualifications:

- Two or more years of teaching experience preferred
- Demonstrated proficiency in the following:
  - teamwork and collaboration
  - curriculum standards

- instructional best practices
- developing assessments of, for, and as learning

Requirements to participate:

- Fulfill all of the responsibilities of your classroom teaching assignment for the year
- A recommendation from the building principal

Responsibilities include but are not limited to the following:

- Attend monthly sessions (during the school day)
- Participate in structured discussions (at monthly sessions and online)
- Apply new learning in the classroom
- Participate in a learning showcase at the end of the year

Transform Academy at a Glance

To launch our Transform Academy, campus principals assisted us in preparing teachers using the pre-session visioning activities presented in Chapter 1. During the first day of the academy, teachers became acquainted with one another, the facilitators, and the overall academy expectations, as described in Chapter 2. The knowledge building continued in subsequent district sessions and field trips, presented in Chapters 3 through 9. Figure I.2 displays the Transform Academy professional learning sessions timeline by month, location, activities, and focus, including the pre-session work conducted by our campus principals.

The sessions identified in Figure I.2 were created to encourage communication, collaboration, and problem solving and to establish a safe learning atmosphere to nurture and nudge our teachers representing a variety of schools. With this in mind, we included ample time for teachers to ask burning questions, dig into the research, and begin formulating their own ideas regarding a learner-centered classroom that cultivates future-ready students. Session plans also included team building, professional book studies, consultant presentations, and field trips to observe innovative learning and work environments. Figure I.2 is also available as Online Resource B.

The online resources cited throughout the book can be accessed at http://resources.corwin.com/MindingTheFuture

Figure I.2 Transform Academy Professional Learning Sessions Timeline

Session & Month	Location	Activities*	Focus
Pre-Session **August**	Participants' campus	1.1 The Future-Ready Classroom 1.2 Visioning for the Future 1.3 Visioning for the Future (alternate activity)	Imagine the classroom of the future. Introduction to visioning tools to be used during the academy.
Session 1 **September**	In academy	2.1 Why Transform? 2.2 Who's Ready? 2.3 A New Vision	Welcome and introduction including purpose, goals, expectations. Develop common understandings and learn more about how visioning impacts transformation.
Session 2 **October**	In academy	3.1 Compass Points 3.2 Building a Tower 3.3 The Power of Yet 3.4 Designing Student Learning Experiences	Build an understanding of personal work styles, increasing teamwork, using mindsets to improve professional and student learning.
Session 3 **November**	In-district field trip to K–8 schools and in academy	4.1 Debriefing Classroom Visits Consultant Presentation(s)	Field trips to observe innovative classrooms. Presentations by instructional and technology consultants.
Session 4 **December**	In-district field trip to high school and in academy	4.2 Debriefing Career and Technical Education Classroom Visits (field trip) Personal Learning Plans (PLPs)	Observe high school course to increase awareness of learning opportunities for students. Begin writing PLPs for implementation and research.
Session 5 **January**	Out-of-district field trip and in academy	Architect Firm PLPs	Learn how workspaces and classrooms are designed. Continue developing PLP and review any implementation progress made.
Session 6 **February**	Out-of-district field trip	Technology Company	Observe at a technology company to understand innovative work environments.
Session 7 **March**	In academy	5.1 What Does It Take to Engage Learners? 5.2 How Does the Environment Affect Learning? PLPs	Discussion and implementation of student voice and choice and the power of flexible learning environments for student growth. Share PLP progress.

(Continued)

Figure I.2 (Continued)

Session & Month	Location	Activities*	Focus
Session 8 **April**	In academy	6.1 Honing Our Craft Learning Fair Presentations	Methods to learn student learning perceptions and preferences. Use PLPs to develop Learning Fair presentations
Session 9 **May**	In academy	Learning Fair 7.1 Leading a Future-Ready Vision	District showcase of instructional innovations and learning during the academy. Discuss next steps and request final participant feedback.

*Activity numbers align with chapter numbering.

Becoming Comfortable With the Unknown

Throughout this book, we offer readers a general guiding process for a new type of professional learning that, based on your academy design, will reveal a variety of new and exciting instructional methods. As our teachers entered the Transform Academy and our facilitation team planned sessions, everyone quickly learned that this was not a typical professional learning opportunity. We found that if an academy's overarching goal is to spark teacher imagination and to implement instructional innovations, then it is important to remember that there will be unintended and unforeseen outcomes. Further, facilitators should desire, expect, and embrace the unknown. For example, we believed that our first academy would bring about teacher requests for new kinds of technology almost exclusively. However, during the year we observed that when given the chance to change the way their classrooms functioned, our teachers were more inspired by numerous other instructional designs and tools. We will describe many of these ideas to you in this book, along with our insights into how we all learned from one another and became comfortable with minding the unknown but exciting future!

With this spirit, we seek *not* to provide you with a recipe for innovative professional learning; rather, we offer you a set of guiding actions to drive teacher-led learning and transformative change. Welcome to the Transform Academy!

CHAPTER 1

Is Your Learning Culture Ready to Transform?

Academy Pre-Session

If you want to go beyond standards and accountability, then where are you going?

ANGELINE A. ANDERSON, SUSAN K. BORG, STEPHANIE L. EDGAR

Getting Acquainted With This Chapter

As teachers and principals prepare to implement a Transform Academy in their school or district, it is important that they examine reliable research about future-ready schools, in addition to collaboratively reviewing the foundational characteristics of their existing learning culture. This chapter introduces readers to the preparatory process during which teachers work together to successfully navigate the transformation process.

Ask the Teachers

Many schools today have mastered their state's "meeting standards" accountability system well enough to be recognized for their efforts. Lights are shining brightly on descriptors such as "exemplary, excellent, clearly outstanding, and A+." Still, there is an uneasy feeling that students, parents, and educators are dissatisfied with defining school as a place to pass annual state assessments and checklists of standards mastered. There appears to be a desire to move beyond the accountability business model of education and, instead, transform the old ways of doing school to something more personal and engaging. Additionally, as a society we are faced with an ever-changing array of new technologies that will influence the future and revolutionize the way we connect with the world. Will our schools be ready to meet the future and the promise it holds?

If school communities want to move beyond standards and accountability, we will need vision, planning, and a learning culture ready for transformation. Our teachers will need to understand the world our students are entering and be ready to create learning environments that support student needs. Our plans must include ways to keep up with the unknown but inevitable technological and societal changes on the horizon and beyond.

Before we look to the future, it is important to acknowledge the foundational components that are currently building strong schools, such as online curricula with learner-driven assessment tools and a continuous professional learning cycle. In addition to these foundational elements, today's teachers collaborate and work in Professional Learning Communities (PLC) using a diverse suite of technology tools to plan differentiated instruction using responsive interventions. We should ask ourselves these questions:

- Are we meeting the needs of our continuously expanding global society?
- Can we assure our community that students will graduate knowing how to collaborate, communicate, create, and think critically?
- Will the learning environment we provide produce future-ready students?

These questions inevitably lead us to the conclusion that we need to change the way that classrooms and schools have traditionally functioned. To find inspiration for designing new schools and classrooms, we look to the latest research findings and models from innovative school districts to show us how we could transform our own schools. We begin to ask ourselves questions, such as,

- Will schools of the future have walls, furniture, bells, and cafeterias?

- Will there continue to be the need for a human connection in learning?

- How do we provide engaging learning for all students for the careers of the future?

The teachers and principals working collaboratively on a daily basis with students will find these answers for themselves—answers that cannot be imposed from outside. When teachers and principals work together in a supportive, collaborative environment while encouraging creativity and risk taking, innovative learning cultures flourish.

As the authors contemplated today's learning landscape, we had another question: "If we want to mind the future, what do we do next?" As we pondered this question over several days, an answer came. The groups needing to be asked this question were our teachers and principals—the practitioners themselves.

To answer the question, "What's next?" not only do we need to ask our most heavily invested stakeholders, we need to ask in a format that leads to learning breakthroughs that encourage creativity and risk taking. This innovative process comes from collaboration with colleagues and exposure to cutting-edge ideas in books, videos, conferences, and field trips. To do this, a novel approach to professional learning is required. We call this model a Transform Academy, and it begins with an intentional, multiyear implementation plan driven by a collaborative learning culture that is ready to study, implement, and ultimately embrace change.

Integrating the strategies resulting from a Transform Academy into a learning culture requires three key aspects to support a successful innovative process: teachers must collaborate and share ideas, participate in profound professional learning activities, and analyze data leading to powerful student success. Few schools have reached perfection in all of the key aspects of a learning culture, so do not let this deter your start of the transformation process. Start with the little things. Small changes will systematically accumulate and result in successful innovative change.

Time to Collaborate!

If you are using this book as a group book study or a small pilot academy, then these sidebars are for you. Before reading about what happened in our academies, try the activities and then compare your thoughts to what we share in the book. As a campus or district group, complete **Activity 1.1 The Future-Ready Classroom**, found at the end of this chapter. Once you have completed the activity together, continue reading the rest of the chapter.

Establishing Your Vision for the Future

We cannot underestimate the importance of supportive, forward-thinking principals who are trailblazers, always ready to take on any challenge and champion ongoing professional learning for student-centered classrooms. These leaders always ask the fundamental question, "What is best for our students?" They know *why* they are proceeding to the next chapter of school improvement and asking others to think differently. These leaders model the actions needed to accomplish change and encourage others to work alongside them in their endeavors.

In preparation for the Transform Academy, we asked participating campus leaders and teachers to complete the pre-session activities found at the end of this chapter and described in the pages that follow. Through these activities, campus teams worked to identify the essential aspects of their learning culture supporting innovation. At the end of the pre-session activities we collected feedback. This information provided guidance to our academy facilitation team as they planned sessions and collected resources for professional learning.

Innovative principals make it a priority to hire and retain teachers who have similar drive and thought processes. When our principals invited teachers to begin studying school transformation using the pre-session activities, teachers, with all their knowledge of learning standards, instructional strategies, and assessment, enthusiastically jumped on board to collaboratively imagine new ways to improve student learning.

After establishing group norms, the campus teams developed a vision of a future-ready classroom, as described in Activity 1.1, to determine the readiness of their school's learning culture to innovate. Once they completed the activity, the teams asked themselves, "Can we meet accountability standards and bring innovative student learning into the same classroom?" The answer was a resounding "YES!"

Time to Collaborate!

Now is a good time to complete **Activity 1.2 Visioning for the Future,** found at the end of this chapter.

Activity 1.2 Visioning for the Future helped principals and their teams identify the essential aspects of their learning culture that support transformation. As we collected feedback from these sessions, we noted commonalities in their work. We found three essential aspects of a learning culture that determine optimal readiness for innovations in student learning: **collaborative communication, professional learning,** and **data collection and planning.**

Essential Aspects of a Learning Culture Ready to Transform

To illustrate the three essential aspects of the readiness of a learning culture to transform, we have created four composite campuses. Each of these campuses represents different levels of readiness to transform.

Collaborative Communication

The first aspect indicating a learning culture is ready to transform is **collaborative communication.** This form of professional communication consists of two parts: **teacher to teacher** and **teacher to principal.**

Collaborative Communication: Teacher to Teacher
• From isolation to collaboration
• Targeted conversations
• Regular intervals
• Principal supported

Our first campus explored developing the effectiveness of their PLC and considered the degree to which *collaborative communication* between teachers existed in their school. For the campus principal and his teachers to steadily move their learning culture from teacher isolation to collaborative responsibility for learners, they know that all teachers must have targeted instructional conversations on a regular basis. The team notes that a PLC or a system of structured teacher collaboration had a less than effective start several years ago. Currently, some teams continue to meet but others are only loosely implementing the PLC process. The team agrees that PLC implementation must become a nonnegotiable expectation. As they discuss renewing this effort, they feel that it is time for specific conversations regarding learning standards and the individual student intervention and enrichment process. *This campus determines that a renewed effort to conduct PLCs with fidelity is needed to eliminate isolation and to communicate an attitude of "we are all in this together" as a cultural necessity for implementing innovative thinking and change in the classrooms.*

Collaborative Communication: Teachers to Principal
• From isolated roles to collaborative responsibility
• Checks the learning progress
• Systematic
• Vertical communication

For several years, the veteran principal at our next campus has valued the PLC process as a communication framework in her campus learning culture. In her search for improvement opportunities she has become interested in emphasizing **collaborative communication between teachers and the principal**. She and her leadership team discuss the importance of systematic vertical collaboration across the faculty to enhance student learning. Her teachers also suggest that the regular exchange of ideas supports the development of a culture of innovation. Thus, her team decides that weekly structured teacher-and-principal meetings will be a high priority. These meetings will include a no interruptions rule and an agenda focused on student learning. *The team agrees that actions from this collaborative opportunity between the teachers and principal contribute to the larger goal of readiness for innovation in the learning culture.*

Professional Learning

Professional Learning
• From standardization to innovation
• Adults are learning all the time
• Prioritizing professional learning

The team at our third campus is part of collaborative data-driven school culture. Throughout her leadership tenure, the principal and her teachers have discussed that an influential feature of learning culture's readiness for innovation is continual **professional learning**. Under the principal's leadership, campus teachers have moved from dreading professional learning to valuing all the relevant training they obtain. As they reflect upon the changes in their learning culture, they describe this positive transition as targeted professional learning that is integrated seamlessly into the collaborative meetings and classrooms. *The team realizes that high quality professional learning supports a learning culture preparing to innovate.*

Data Collection and Planning

Data Collection and Planning
• From standardization to innovation
• Regularly collected student data
• Results inform instruction
• Instruction is student focused

During their leadership meetings, the fourth principal and his teachers discussed the importance of systematic student **data collection and planning** within their learning culture. As the team reviews their current status, they realize this is an area in need of improvement. Along with his team, he establishes an expectation of data collection and planning for the purpose of developing informed instructional decisions within the collaborative learning culture. *The team reflects that once the student data discussions and systematic planning became part of the language of the learning culture, innovative thinking regarding student-centered learning processes followed.*

Transformation-minded principals like the ones described above know that the readiness drivers supporting innovative instructional practices include teacher-to-teacher collaboration, systematic teacher-leader interaction, relevant adult learning, and data collection for comprehensive planning. As a result, trust between all professionals improves, teachers and the principal support one another, and continued, high-quality professional learning becomes "the way we do things around here." Learning among the adults becomes just as essential as the student learning outcomes. Transformation is just around the corner!

Framework for Transforming a Learning Culture

Figure 1.1 Framework for Transforming a Learning Culture summarizes the key aspects leading to **transformational learning**. On the top of the framework, the **driving vision** for transformation is fueled by the opposing societal forces of governmental mandates for standardization and the grassroots efforts of educators craving innovation. These forces

Figure 1.1 Framework for Transforming a Learning Culture

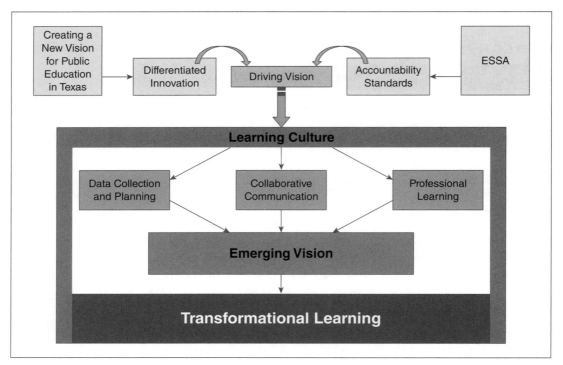

propel teachers to focus on what is best for their students and implement innovative learning practices supported by the learning culture. As principals and teachers examine the readiness of their learning culture, they also use data to find areas in need of improvement and collaboratively plan to research instructional best practices and tools. This information further guides **professional learning**. Through **collaborative communication** and professional learning, along with **data collection and planning,** an emerging vision develops and leads to transformational learning. It is here that student engagement and learning outcomes are advanced by empowered teacher voices. Throughout this book, we will reference the framework in Figure 1.1 as we explore the transformation of learning cultures.

Planning and Chronicling Your Transform Academy

Whether you are implementing a districtwide or campus-based Transform Academy, systematic action planning is essential to develop a learning culture for innovative thinking. Further, documentation of your work and achievements will sustain the project as it progresses. As you define the focus of your academy, it is important to develop action plans that provide a step-by-step guide and evidence-based performance indicators to monitor progress. A calendar will help keep the team on track. If you use the calendar to review plans—as well as a journal—it will be easier to celebrate achievements and record redirections taken in the action steps.

Here are some helpful tips to start the planning process and spark your thinking.

- An achievable plan starts with a vision
- Develop a needs assessment that also includes cultural readiness and strengths
- Set goals and actionable steps with evidence such as achievement measures
- Set timelines and place them on a shared calendar

Remember to keep working with your plan, document progress, and keep it flexible. Plans today are written digitally, so nothing is written in stone—that went out with the cave tablets!

Online Resource C provides a checklist to assist you in answering the question, "Is your learning culture ready to transform?" This resource provides you with a series of questions relating to the three supportive aspects of a learning culture preparing to innovate: collaborative communication, professional learning, and data collection and planning. To this checklist we have also added a brief survey of technological readiness. These questions will help you determine the current status of your technology tools and infrastructure. The checklist is provided as an editable document online so that you can easily adapt the questions to match the particular needs of your school community.

Differentiated Approaches for Professional Learning

As leaders review readiness to implement innovative ideas, they may begin by determining how to approach transforming a learning culture in their respective districts or schools. Their approaches will be varied and differentiated and may include a full Transform Academy, small pilots, and book studies.

Academy

While there is no "one way" to plan for a year-long professional learning experience, it often helps to learn from others who have been involved in a similar experience. Here we offer our work. A set of activities designed to spark professional learning and encourage innovation can be found at the end of the chapters. These activities engage learners, stimulate conversations, and make participant thinking visible. An action orientation should result from this type of learning experience. While targeted professional learning experiences should be aligned to the needs of the group, the end-of-chapter activities may be utilized as provided or serve as a springboard for a more personalized experience.

Pilot Study

We recommend starting your Transform Academy as a small pilot in the first year to understand how the work will unfold. This will also give you room to reflect and make adjustments to the plan early in the implementation. Celebrate your successes often and address any concerns as soon as possible. Remember to plan for regular updates to the campus, district personnel, and the community. Put these updates on your calendar and follow up to give both the team and the Transform Academy credibility. By keeping an emphasis on your initiative through planning, monitoring, evaluating, and reporting, you are highlighting accomplishments and potentially avoiding participant and organizational fatigue.

Book Study

Though your district or school may have a collaborative communication framework in place, you may not be ready to implement a professional learning plan on the scale of the Transform Academy. A different professional learning format may need to be employed. Collaborative teams led by the campus principal may use this book to examine transformation and to start thinking about how this process works. The Time to Collaborate! sidebars and Discussion Questions in each chapter are starting point opportunities for teachers and leadership teams to collectively share their thinking about transforming teaching and learning. This process will provide a learning environment that nurtures collaboration and communication between teachers and campus leaders.

To guide readers with any of these undertakings, an action item checklist is available at the end of each chapter. Please adapt these resources to meet your needs.

At the conclusion of each chapter, we offer the reader a summary of key ideas followed by discussion questions, activity descriptions, and action items to guide the work outlined in the chapter. In Chapter 1, the importance of bringing teacher voice into the leadership team is emphasized along with the essential aspects of leading a learning culture preparing to transform. Pre-session activities to inspire innovative professional development are integrated into a team's work to determine the readiness of a learning culture to transform.

DISCUSSION QUESTIONS

1. What is the meaning of *future ready*?

2. As a leadership team, schoolwide team, or district team, develop a working definition of *future ready* to serve as a foundation for discussions.

3. How does the current culture of the campus or district support this type of professional learning?

4. Who would need to be included in the conversations to move forward with this type of professional learning?

Transform Academy Pre-Session Activities

The activities that follow describe the pre-session work completed by our campus principals and their leadership team prior to the start of the Transform Academy Session 1.

ACTIVITY 1.1 THE FUTURE-READY CLASSROOM

Intended Outcome: To develop a personal definition and vision of the future-ready classroom

Please visit http://resources.corwin.com/MindingTheFuture to access the online resources for this book.

Preparation: chart paper, markers, scissors, colored pencils, construction paper (or a variety of colored sheets of paper), glue sticks, tape, sticky notes

Facilitator Note: One of the goals of Chapter 1 is for the reader to develop a clear understanding of the term *future ready* and to be able to explain why it is important for students. Once individuals develop their own understanding of what it means to be future ready, it is just as important that campuses and districts develop a common understanding of future ready to ensure that all stakeholders are moving toward the same vision. At the end of the activity, be sure to save the group definition and vision chart for further use as participants refine their vision of a future-ready classroom over time.

Facilitation:

1. Facilitator asks: What is the meaning of *future ready*? Individual participants develop their own working definition of *future ready* to serve as a foundation for discussions.

2. The facilitator continues the activity by posing the next question: What would a future-ready classroom look like?

3. Individual participants or teams use the materials provided to create an image of the future-ready classroom they envision.

4. In groups of four to six colleagues, participants share their creations and explain why the components are critical in the classroom of the future.

5. Mount the images on the walls and ask participants to walk around the room to view the images created by other groups, making notes of recurring components.

6. Participants return to their table groups and begin discussing the similar components found on the charts. Each table group creates a list of the components that should be included in a future-ready classroom.

7. The facilitator guides a whole-group discussion that results in a vision chart containing the campus or district definition and vision of the future-ready classroom.

ACTIVITY 1.2 VISIONING FOR THE FUTURE

Intended Outcome: To discuss the factors that contribute to the development of an emerging vision and transformational learning

Preparation: chart paper, sticky notes

Facilitator Note: This activity is intended to initiate a conversation and thinking about the connections between vision, culture, and transformational learning.

Facilitation:

1. The facilitator begins the activity by asking participants to reflect on the following questions:

   - What is our campus vision for learning?
   - What aspects of our learning culture would support transformational learning?
   - What processes and systems do we have in place that would support the changes that could result in transformation?

2. Working in small groups, the participants begin to discuss their thoughts related to the questions. The individual responses are written on sticky notes.

3. Each table group pairs with another table group and begins to discuss the responses on the sticky notes. As they share the responses they should begin to form categories of responses and label the categories.

4. Once all sticky notes for each group have been placed in categories, the facilitator pulls the group together.

5. The facilitator questions the groups about the categories that were created based on their responses. The facilitator records the labels for the groups on a large chart that all participants can see. Members from each group place the individual sticky notes in the appropriate categories.

6. After the facilitator shares the responses in each category, the facilitator asks the following questions: What do you notice? What connections can be made? Why is this information important?

7. The participants reflect on the questions and determine next steps.

ACTIVITY 1.3 VISIONING FOR THE FUTURE (ALTERNATE ACTIVITY)

Intended Outcome: To discuss the factors that contribute to the development of an emerging vision and transformational learning

Preparation: Online Resource D.1 (this is a digital version of Figure 1.1 Framework for Transforming a Learning Culture), individual copies of Online Resource D.2, index cards

Facilitator Note: Activity 1.3 can be used in place of Activity 1.2.

Facilitation:

1. The facilitator begins the activity by displaying Resource D.1 and providing the following directions to initiate the activity: You will have two minutes to silently view this chart. As you do so, keep the following questions in mind:

   - What do you notice?
   - What connections can be made?
   - Why is this information important?

2. Participants independently complete the Visioning for the Future handout (Resource D.2), responding to the questions in each section.

3. Working with table partners, the participants trade handouts and review the responses. Once the partners have read the responses, they should share their thinking regarding their responses to the questions.

4. The facilitator directs each set of partners to find a set of partners from another table. Once the group of four is created, the new partners trade handouts and review the responses. Once again, the four group members share their thinking regarding their responses to the questions.

5. The participants return to their original tables and record any new ideas or information on their individual handouts.

6. Displaying Resource D.1, the facilitator provides the following prompt: After reflecting on the information on the chart and sharing it with partners, my next step is _____. Participants write their responses to the prompt on individual index cards and submit them to the facilitator.

Suggested Action Items

Action Items	Progress Checks			
1. Determine the professional learning format you will be using for this text:				
• Use the book for self-study	☐ Not started	☐ In progress	☐ Completed	☐ NA
• Start with a small pilot team to study each chapter and make plans for a future implementation	☐ Not started	☐ In progress	☐ Completed	☐ NA
• Form a leadership team in order to begin a Transform Academy of an appropriate scale for your needs	☐ Not started	☐ In progress	☐ Completed	☐ NA
2. Prioritize your needs and utilize the professional learning activities in this chapter.				
• Discussion Questions	☐ Not started	☐ In progress	☐ Completed	☐ NA
• Activity 1.1 The Future-Ready Classroom	☐ Not started	☐ In progress	☐ Completed	☐ NA
• Activity 1.2 Visioning for the Future	☐ Not started	☐ In progress	☐ Completed	☐ NA
• or Activity 1.3 (alternate activity)	☐ Not started	☐ In progress	☐ Completed	☐ NA
3. Prioritize your needs and utilize the resources provided in this chapter.				
• Resource C. Is Your Learning Culture Ready to Transform?	☐ Not started	☐ In progress	☐ Completed	☐ NA
4. Determine how you or your team will document your work by developing calendars for study, meeting, journaling, data checks, and communicating results.	☐ Not started	☐ In progress	☐ Completed	☐ NA

CHAPTER 2

Developing Collaborative Innovators

Session 1

Find a great school and I will show you a school where decision making is shared and teachers are empowered to lead.

—STEPHANIE HIRSH

- -

Getting Acquainted With This Chapter

There is no one way to transform, so the key to this successful professional learning process is found in teacher collaboration. In this chapter, getting comfortable with being uncomfortable is necessary because supportive facilitation of innovative thinking creates student-centered learning classrooms. The transition from working in isolation to collaboration and from standardized learning to innovative experiences empowers teachers to transform learning environments and ultimately develops teams of collaborative innovators ready to personalize student learning.

- -

Culture of Innovation:
How Do You Define It?

Ten years ago, a group of forward-thinking school district superintendents in Texas assembled to discuss what they thought schools should be addressing when planning for the classrooms of the future. These innovative superintendents produced a document that continues to drive the work of many school districts today. They assembled five articles containing groundbreaking thoughts and research describing *the new digital learning environment, the new learning standards, assessment for learning, accountability for learning, and organizational transformation.* This visionary document was titled *Creating a New Vision for Public Education in Texas.* Its words inspired educational leaders by giving them a roadmap to create new ways to approach learning, assessment, and organizational transformation (Texas Association of School Administrators [TASA], 2008). This resource and others like it across the United States and Canada, such as *Shifting Minds 3.0: Redefining the Learning Landscape in Canada* (Milton, 2015), *Preparing 21st Century Students for a Global Society* (National Education Association, 2015), and *Framework for 21st Century Learning* (Partnership for 21st Century Learning, 2015), became a catalyst for stimulating discussion about the changing classroom landscape. The transformative thinking outlined in these guiding resources gives leaders permission to go beyond standards-based accountability and return passion to teaching and learning. We recommend beginning your Transform Academy process with a comparable resource to inspire and inform your school community and to provide a common basis from which to start your rich discussions.

The first five articles of the *Creating a New Vision for Public Education in Texas* provided a visionary guide for our academy work. They brought clarity to the transformation process as we moved from standardized teaching to innovational learning. In the examples below, we have provided a sample driving question and a corresponding transformation target for each article. Transformation targets represent ideal outcomes upon completion of the implementation options. Keep in mind that driving questions, transformation targets, and implementation options will differ as teams consider each article and determine their current realities. The thoughts presented are a composite of the work of our teachers and principals. This information is also presented in table form in Online Resource E and is meant to be a flexible tool for your visioning work.

Time to Collaborate!

Now is a good time to complete **Activity 2.1 Why Transform?** found at the end of this chapter.

Digital Learning Environment

Article I of the visioning document (TASA, 2008) addresses "The New Digital Learning Environment." An example driving question for this article is "What is the current status of digital learning in our district/school?" A corresponding transformation target would be "To develop a long-term plan to intensify the integration of digital devices into a learning culture." Implementation options include long-term projects such as

- implementing digital learning networks
- using digital resources for learning
- exploring new technologies
- meaningful use of the devices and resources
- educating the community about the use of digital devices in the classroom

New Learning Standards

Article II conveys the need for "New Learning Standards" that capture the values and capabilities needed for a global world (TASA, 2008). A related driving question may be, "How does our PLC structure implement a deeper approach to learning standards with instructional strategies that embrace the whole child?" An aligned transformation target would state, "Extend our current learning standards to include connected and applicable learning experiences." Below are possible implementation options:

- set clear, attainable, motivating standards
- assure that standards are achieved at a profound level
- develop learning standards that embrace the whole child
- assure that lessons support multiple intelligences/imagination/ curiosity
- use digital devices to make learning relevant to students

Assessment for Learning

Article III, "Assessment for Learning," may yield a driving question such as, "How do we ensure successful student outcomes with a variety of assessment tools?" (TASA, 2008). A corresponding transformation target may state, "Use authentic formative and summative assessments to inform students of progress in a timely manner." This article challenges teachers and their principals to consider the following implementation options:

- use continuous assessments for, as, and of learning
- develop a variety of assessments outside of the multiple-choice realm
- vary feedback to the students and parents
- practice authentic, meaningful assessment

Accountability for Learning

Article IV, "Accountability for Learning," may produce a driving question such as, "How can we implement an accountability system that places less emphasis on standardized testing and focuses on what our community values?" (TASA, 2008). A transformation target for this question may read, "Design an accountability system for our district/campus that uses multiple measures, varied assessments, and clear reporting methods." Implementation options for this article include the following:

- report other assessment results along with the state assessments
- report the results of long-term measures such as college completion rates
- broaden the valued areas of accountability beyond standardized tests

Organizational Transformation

Article V, "Organizational Transformation," moves us to a driving question such as, "How can we improve our learning culture through authentic and personalized professional development opportunities?" (TASA, 2008). A commensurate transformation target may state, "Institute a professional development program to encourage teacher voice in leadership." This article invites school innovation teams to

- commit to higher levels of student engagement
- transition the teacher role to a designer of engaging learning experiences
- develop ways to support all teachers and leaders to change the way the school approaches learning so that profound learning is occurring

The visioning document (TASA, 2008) we used is just one of several research tools for exploring the possibilities for innovative change on your campus. Facilitation teams may wish to explore a variety of resources (i.e., books, conferences/conventions, articles, and guest speakers) as they examine innovative ways to improve student engagement in learning.

As our academy teachers examined the possibilities for transformation outlined in the visioning resources, they found that readiness for innovation is essential. The teams agreed that a grassroots effort meant to transform learning required participants prepared for a roller coaster of emotions. Paving the way for revolutionary ways of thinking and doing is not easy in a standardized world. Participation in learning through the Transform Academy involved courage and risk-taking, failures and triumphs as the teachers began to engage in innovative thinking. For example, as the year progressed, several of teachers courageously started to change their physical learning environments based on their new learning. They added comfortable seating like bean bags, stools, and pillows; rugs to define reading areas; lowered tables so students could sit on the floor; and placed fewer desks in the room, all in an effort to offer personal choice and comfort to students. Another teacher allowed students to choose their seat each day, and she no longer had absence or tardy issues that previously impacted the learning environment. Yet another teacher asked her students what would make her a better teacher, and she received a wealth of feedback ranging from selecting different ways and times to complete assignments, changes in assessments, and opportunities for digital group work. It was difficult for her to accept their feedback at first, but she gradually implemented their suggestions with increasing success. At every academy session, teachers shared their experiences with the ideas that they tried. The students became their partners in the change as they, too, desired a place in school that was engaging and fun.

Time to Collaborate!

Now is a good time to complete **Activity 2.2 Who's Ready?** found at the end of this chapter.

Becoming a Collaborative Innovator

As we examined readiness for transformation, we found two overarching principles needed for successful instructional transformation. These principles demonstrate that when empowered by involvement in innovative thinking and professional learning, teachers tend to grow in two directions. This growth is illustrated using the quadrant chart in Figure 2.1. Along the horizontal axis we see Principle I: In an optimal learning culture, teachers move from Isolation to Collaboration. Along the vertical axis Principle II is found: In an optimal learning culture, teachers move from Standardization to Innovation. Using examples of teacher thinking and voice allows us to understand how teachers fall into each quadrant along the way to becoming collaborative innovators.

Figure 2.1 Voices of Teachers Growing Toward Collaborative Innovation

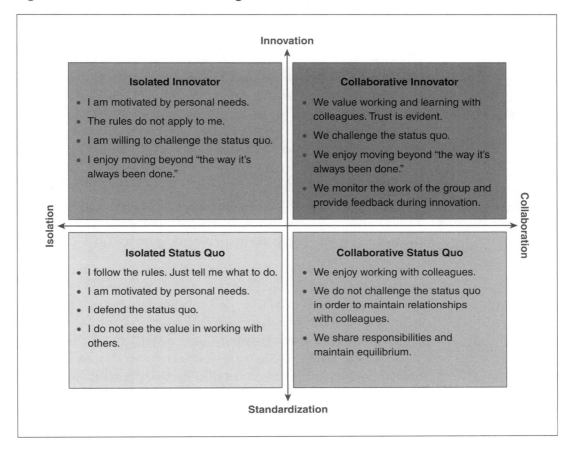

Voices of Teachers in Transition

Upon closer examination of the individual quadrants, we find that a teacher who is isolated and focused solely on standardization is designated as "isolated status quo." This teacher follows the rules, wants to be told what to do, is motivated by personal needs, defends standardization, and does not see value in working with others. This person may be stuck in a rut and not wish to change because of the additional work change may bring.

As a teacher gives up the personal need for isolation and moves toward the "collaborative status quo," he enjoys working with others, but still does not challenge the standardization that has become part of his learning culture. This teacher shares responsibilities but wants to maintain the current equilibrium and not rock the boat.

When the isolated status quo teacher does some research on his own but keeps it to himself, he moves into the "isolated innovator" quadrant.

He is willing to change the status quo and enjoys moving beyond the way things have always been done. Yet he remains in isolation and simply becomes a small pocket of innovation in the bigger learning culture.

When the need for systematic collaboration and innovative learning come together, then the collaborative innovator is born! This teacher values working and learning with his colleagues. He develops trust with others and begins to challenge the status quo by moving beyond the way things have always been done. He holds the group and himself accountable and provides and accepts feedback during innovation. This is the pinnacle of transition for both principles. When this voice and behavior are present in a majority of the teachers in a learning culture, their emerging vision is driven toward transformational learning. Teacher leaders who act as collaborative innovators can go a long way toward revitalizing their school's learning culture.

When a team examines the progress of individuals and the campus in general using these principles, it is possible to determine the status of a learning culture moving toward collaborative innovation. Could there be pockets of transformational thinking happening throughout a school and district? Absolutely, but one purpose of a Transform Academy is to create a systematic way to transition the most people forward. Ideally, this progression will collectively move individuals in positive directions resulting in collaborative innovation.

In our experience, analyzing the visioning document (TASA, 2008) caused many educators to reflect about how they were affecting student outcomes. As research and reflection integrated into collaborative meetings and eventually into classrooms, transitions occurred in individual teachers as well as the entire learning culture. Isolation decreased and collaboration increased, while standardization shifts to the background and innovative thinking began to move front and center. This caused a ripple effect over the school as students noticed that something different but wonderful was happening.

Using what we just learned, let's explore Day 1 of the Transform Academy. We will share with you what happened and how to implement the activities we used to encourage our teachers to begin their visioning for the future.

Professional Learning for
Transform Academy Session 1

As we began our journey with teachers the energy level was incredible—and so was the apprehension. Teachers were thrilled to have the opportunity to be involved in an endeavor called Transform Academy. They were proud their principals had selected them as participants. But, they were anxious that they would not be able to meet the expectations of their principals. Actually, they were not really sure about what they had agreed to, and the anticipation of coming expectations was on their minds.

On the first day of the Transform Academy, our initial contact with the teachers was quite memorable. They walked into the room like excited students on the first day of school, looking around the room to find a friend to ease their anxiety. Little did they know that the facilitators were feeling the same way. There was a buzz in the room that would signify something important was about to happen.

As they settled into table groups with colleagues from their campuses, we could hear the conversations. What is this about? Why am I here? What do you think we will be learning? Are we the only ones in this group? These were some of the questions they pondered prior to starting what would become a transformational year for everyone involved. It seemed odd to us they were so worried about why they were the "chosen ones" for this new endeavor.

We, too, were asking ourselves questions. Did we plan this initial day of Transform Academy in a way that would be engaging and relevant to each of them? Did we arrange activities so that we would be modeling the type of learning experiences we hoped they would utilize in their classrooms? What if things do not go well today and they decide they do not want to participate in this academy? Do *we* know enough to facilitate this year-long professional development plan? Have we organized the learning to align with the district's vision?

Let the Transformation Begin!

We began our day as the teachers introduced themselves to the group. Those of us facilitating the day of learning were trying to remember as much as we could about each teacher. We needed them to know that we were going to be collaborative partners in this learning process. Since the teachers' principals were invited to attend this initial day of Transform Academy, they introduced themselves and proudly stated the names of their teachers in attendance. The superintendent, along with other central office administrators, greeted the teachers and shared their excitement about this new endeavor. Their presence signified the importance of this journey we had embarked upon as well as their commitment to each teacher's success along the way.

It was interesting to watch and listen to the teachers' responses as the introductions proceeded. They commented they had heard many of our names, even received emails from some of us, but never really knew who we were. They were glad to match our faces to our names.

Prior to the introductions of the teachers, principals, and central office staff, we had placed a slide up for view in the room. The slide included actions participants needed to complete before the start of the session: make a name tent for the table, create a Twitter account, and download a QR code reader. This was our first opportunity to assess our learners.

Once the introductions were completed, we moved into Activity 2.1 Why Transform? The intent was to engage the participants in thinking about why transformation in teaching and learning needed to occur. We thought this would help answer some of their burning questions of why they were there. It worked! For some of the teachers, this was their first time using a QR code reader. With comments like "I'm going to use this in my classroom tomorrow" and "I could do this with my students for a review before a test," we knew we were off to a good start. We also knew that we needed to provide opportunities for them to learn about other technology tools that would transfer to classroom use.

Prior to our mid-morning break, we provided the teachers with a quick introduction to the learning management tool we would be using throughout the year. Although not everyone was familiar with this online learning platform, those who were familiar began supporting their colleagues. We had begun to build a culture of collaboration.

Why Should We Change?

It was time for a history lesson. We needed to provide a brief historical perspective of public education in American culture in order to set the context for change. We were compelled to discuss the need for transformation in education as well as possible areas of transformation. We wondered if the teachers would feel comfortable expressing their opinions and frustrations since this was only the morning of Day 1 of Transform Academy. We did not need to worry. They were articulate and passionate as they shared their feelings about accountability at the state and district levels. Fostering a student-centered learning environment that would develop future-ready students was important to each of them, but they felt as though their hands were tied. There were too many standards for teaching demanded by the state, which prevented them from providing learning experiences that allowed students to go deeper with their learning. The amount of testing was discouraging, as well as the format of testing. Assessments that revealed students' capacities beyond multiple-choice tests were needed.

Later, as we reflected on the first day of Transform Academy, it seemed this was the defining moment. They had been honest about what they wanted to see changed in our local education system, but past experiences caused them to doubt that it could really happen. The way we responded to their comments was critical. It was time for us to hear the teachers' voices and support them as they began to change teaching and learning in their classrooms.

Who Is Ready to Change?

Change can be difficult, and this magnitude of change was going to require attention and probably lots of nurturing along the way. Activity 2.2 Who's Ready? was designed to get the teachers talking about the kinds of change educators encounter as they work toward collaborative innovation. The activity chart labeled isolation, collaboration, standardization, and innovation (Figure 2.1) sparked conversation, particularly the standardization and isolation quadrants. Once they were provided with the labels for the four types of teachers and asked to start identifying the characteristics, they had much more to say. They all knew of someone who had the characteristics of the isolated status quo. They made comments like, "There's a teacher on my team just like this! She never wants to meet with us to plan and always finds an excuse to miss our planning sessions." In each quadrant of the chart they were able to make a connection between the characteristics they had identified and a teacher on their campus. As they completed this activity, they began to recognize why they were the "chosen ones."

The Dreaming Begins

So far, Day 1 of Transform Academy had been engaging and full of thoughtful conversation and dreaming about what could be. We had provided opportunities for them to communicate, collaborate, and think critically with this new group of colleagues that would become more than just another professional learning cohort. It was evident the participants experienced a learning culture that supported authentic professional growth in their schools. The teachers were extremely collaborative and thus had one of the attributes necessary for transformational change. The final activity for the day, Activity 2.3 A New Vision, created the most exhilarating dialogue from the teachers and provided the most insight for the facilitators. As they worked their way through the various articles of the visioning document (TASA, 2008), they were intrigued by the content and excited at the prospect of being part of a grassroots effort to bring this type of change to classrooms. As we listened to conversations in the small groups, we heard comments such as, "Why haven't we seen this before? Are they really going to let us change the way we look at the standards? Do you really think they'll let us use technology in this way?" One of the most important things we learned during this activity was that some teachers truly believed that we, central office administrators, were the force holding them back and keeping them from moving forward in their work. As we reflected on our plan for the year, we had to make sure that we had included opportunities for central office staff to engage in some of the activities with the teachers. In addition to everything we hoped to accomplish, we needed to focus on developing trusting relationships within this larger learning community.

KEY iDEAS

In this chapter, we emphasized the importance of the readiness of the learning culture to provide a foundation for successful school transformation efforts. Another impactful strategy of the transformation process involves developing a driving question during project design. As Transform Academy Session 1 concluded, it was evident that teacher voice drives the goals of the project, with the ultimate outcome of developing collaborative innovators in the learning environment.

DISCUSSION QUESTIONS

1. As a leadership team, how will you determine who is ready for this journey?

2. How will the leadership team and teachers determine which research to study?

3. How will you communicate the work of this team of teachers and administrators to other teachers on campus, parents, and district leaders?

Transform Academy Session 1 Activities

ACTIVITY 2.1 WHY TRANSFORM?

Intended Outcome: To engage participants in thinking about *why* transformation of teaching and learning is critical

Preparation: Prepare cards using quotes from Online Resource F

Facilitator Note: When constructing the cards for this activity, be careful to use the same QR code with the name of the author for each half of the quote. This provides a means of self-checking.

Facilitation:

1. The facilitator provides the following directions for the activity: Each participant will receive one part of a quote. The goal is to find the person with the part of a quote that completes your quote. Use the QR code to identify the author of the quote and to confirm the match.

2. Distribute a card to each participant.

3. Participants walk around the room in search of the match to their part of the quote.

4. With their matching partner, participants discuss the quote and its relevance to transformation.

5. In a large group, each pair of participants shares their quote and its relevance in the transformation process.

6. The facilitator summarizes the participants' ideas as well as the connections to why transformation of teaching and learning is critical.

ACTIVITY 2.2 WHO'S READY?

Intended Outcome: To communicate their thoughts and ideas regarding the kind of teacher movement required in order to develop a future-ready culture of learning

Preparation: index cards, sticky notes, markers, chart paper, pens/pencils

Facilitator Note: One intended outcome of this chapter is for the reader to develop an understanding of the kind of teacher movement needed in order

Please visit http://resources.corwin.com/MindingTheFuture to access the online resources for this book.

to successfully develop a future-ready culture at the campus/district level. The facilitator will want to keep the four charts for further use as participants learn more about the four quadrants and the characteristics of the teachers within each quadrant.

It is important to note this activity could be completed using digital tools instead of charts, index cards, and sticky notes. Keep in mind that collaboration, communication, critical thinking, and creativity are key factors in this transformational process, and planning for professional learning should allow for this to occur.

Facilitation:

1. The facilitator begins the activity by displaying Online Resource G and inviting comments regarding the four indicators of movement: isolation, collaboration, standardization, and innovation.

2. In groups of four to six, participants discuss the types of teachers that correspond to the four quadrants on the chart, in order to clarify the desired movement of teachers in a future-ready environment. On the four index cards they write the following labels: isolated status quo, collaborative status quo, isolated innovator, and collaborative innovator.

3. Using sticky notes, each group develops a list of characteristics that correspond to each of the four types of teachers. The list may also contain typical questions that a teacher in the particular quadrant might ask. Place the sticky notes under the appropriate index card to create the four quadrants.

4. The facilitator places four charts on the wall, each chart labeled with one of the types of teachers. Participants at each table are directed to place the sticky notes created by each group on the corresponding chart on the wall.

5. The facilitator selects two participants per chart to group notes that are similar. This will expedite the next step in the process.

6. The facilitator reads the sticky notes on the Isolated Status Quo chart and then provides an opportunity for further discussion and clarification. The facilitator completes the same process on the Collaborative Status Quo chart, followed by the Isolated Innovator and the Collaborative Innovator. As each chart is discussed, the participants will begin clarifying their thinking about each quadrant. As a result, some of the attributes on the charts might need to be revised.

7. The facilitator seeks input from the participants to create a summary of the learning.

ACTIVITY 2.3 A NEW VISION

Intended Outcome: To study *Creating a New Vision for Public Education in Texas* and determine a focus for their study during this year-long academy

Preparation: individual copies of *Creating a New Vision for Public Education in Texas* (see Online Resource H).

Facilitator Note: Although we selected *Creating a New Vision for Public Education in Texas,* your team may decide to utilize a different document. The steps outlined below relate directly to our study of our visioning document (TASA, 2008). We created a digital document that contained the questions located at the end of each article. This allowed the participants to respond to the questions and provided access to the document for the entire group.

Facilitation:

1. The facilitator begins the activity by asking the following questions:

   - Why do we need to transform teaching and learning in our school?

   - How do you envision future-ready teaching and learning in our school?

   - How would that be different from our current reality?

2. In small groups, the participants discuss the three questions. The facilitator provides an opportunity for each group to share their responses with the entire group.

3. The facilitator provides each participant with a copy of *Creating a New Vision for Public Education in Texas*. The participants number off from 1 to 5. The numbers align with five of the six articles from the visioning document (TASA, 2008) presented at the beginning of the chapter. The participants then move to designated areas of the room based on the assigned article.

4. Each group member silently reads the Statement of Principle and Supporting Premises sections, recording reflections and/or questions she or he has regarding each section. As a group, they discuss their reflections and then respond to the following questions on the digital document:

   If we embraced this principle and its supporting premises,

   - What changes might we expect to see?

     o In students?

     o In the environment in which teachers and students work?

     o In the focus of our actions?

- What new capacities will we need and how will we develop them?

- How would embracing this principle impact our beliefs, bringing greater clarity to our sense of direction and what we want to be like five years from now?

5. When all groups have completed the assigned section, the facilitator leads the group through a review of each section, allowing members from the section being reviewed to share their thoughts regarding the responses.

6. The facilitator asks the group the following question: Now that you have reviewed the visioning document (TASA, 2008), which article or articles do you think we need to study as we envision future-ready teaching and learning in our schools? Allow participants to share their thoughts before coming to consensus on the article/articles of focus for the year.

Suggested Action Items

Action Items	Progress Checks			
1. Review the steps you took after reading Chapter 1. Make planning adjustments and communication updates as needed.	☐ Not started	☐ In progress	☐ Completed	☐ NA
2. Prioritize your needs and complete the professional learning activities in this chapter.				
• Discussion Questions	☐ Not started	☐ In progress	☐ Completed	☐ NA
• Activity 2.1 Why Transform?	☐ Not started	☐ In progress	☐ Completed	☐ NA
• Activity 2.2 Who's Ready?	☐ Not started	☐ In progress	☐ Completed	☐ NA
• Activity 2.3 A New Vision	☐ Not started	☐ In progress	☐ Completed	☐ NA
3. Review calendars for study, meeting, journaling, data checks, and communicating results.	☐ Not started	☐ In progress	☐ Completed	☐ NA

CHAPTER 3

Teacher Voice

Session 2

Teacher voice is about listening to others, learning from what is being said, and leading by taking action together.

—RUSSELL QUAGLIA AND LISA LANDE

Getting Acquainted With This Chapter

Change in the learning environment begins with a partnership between teachers who are interested in improving student engagement. The prominence of a collaborative teacher voice in the transformative process, supported by the principal, results in an emerging vision for the learning culture of the school. This chapter highlights how together teachers use research to inform their practice, which results in a variety of innovations in the classroom.

Celebrating Teacher Innovation

Sometimes it is interesting to think about an outcome you envision upon completing a process. If we fast forward to the end of the school year, we find the superintendent as he pays a visit to a Transform Academy first grade classroom. He is ushered into a learning environment where students take his hand and eagerly explain that they are doing project-based learning. They are studying examples of how animals camouflage themselves in various habitats and then proposing ways for animals of their choice to camouflage themselves in a city. The superintendent, wearing a crisp white shirt with his gray suit, bravely sits on a wobbly stool while the students hand him one of their new digital tablets. Their quick fingers show him what areas to click on the colorful screens so he can view their collaborative projects incorporating creativity and critical thinking. Other students in the classroom are busily going about the business of learning in small groups, using various seating arrangements throughout the room and spilling into the hallway. Our superintendent is mesmerized by the student engagement and excitement. He asks the teacher, "What have you learned that has caused the students to be so independent and engaged in learning?" The answer comes with a description of the teacher's personal year-long journey in the Transform Academy and how this professional learning opportunity has given her fresh eyes and a new perspective about how students learn. Further, she explains the importance of having an "all students will achieve growth" mindset when creating innovative learning environments. The superintendent gratefully agrees and promises to sustain the momentum of the Transform Academy in the years ahead for minding the future.

When we consider innovation in education, we should remember that teachers have been practicing this idea since the beginnings of the profession. Think about the ingenious ways they use milk crates, rubber bands, poster board, tennis balls, and construction paper to build learning events. It is easy to see why most teachers revel in being creative. Some creations are inspired by necessity due to changing standards and budget cuts, while others are stimulated through professional dialogue, research, and technology. In the best cases, innovation is energized by collaborative, action-oriented professional learning and can lead to a collaborative innovator mindset. This type of adult learning validates existing proficiencies, creates venues for professional sharing, builds upon our natural desire to learn, and provides a means for applying new knowledge and skills. When this happens in a place where it is safe to voice differing perspectives and share concerns, we begin celebrating breakthroughs in teacher leadership and student success.

Three Components of an Emerging Vision

As described in Chapters 1 and 2, the Transform Academy was created to encourage and honor revolutionary instructional practices in a

Figure 3.1 Excerpt From the Framework for Transforming a Learning Culture: Emerging Vision

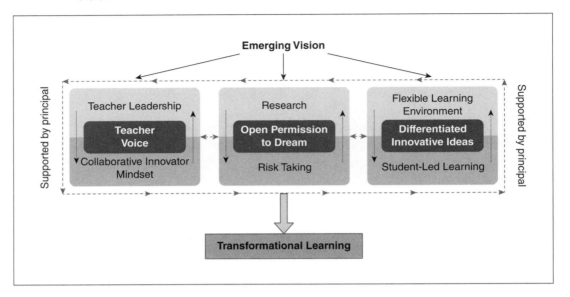

collaborative learning culture using project-based learning (see Figure I.1 in the Introduction). The idea that teachers would move from standardized classroom operations to shared innovation built around new ways of thinking and doing requires a professional learning approach driven by a new vision, teacher-led professional learning, a commitment to collaborate, and planning to meet personal goals. From this an emerging vision develops, ultimately leading to transformational learning.

Figure 3.1 is an expansion of the emerging vision section of Figure 1.1 Framework for Transforming a Learning Culture introduced in Chapter 1. When the emerging vision is closely examined, three key components appear to benefit and stimulate the creation of new ways to learn and work: encouraging **teacher voice**, giving **open permission to dream**, and developing **differentiated innovative ideas**.

We will begin our discussion in this chapter by briefly exploring how each of the components of an emerging vision cultivate excitement and innovative thinking in a Transform Academy setting. Then we will take a closer look at teacher voice. In Chapter 4, we will explore open permission to dream. Following Chapter 4, we will spend time in a deeper exploration of differentiated innovative ideas, including flexible learning environment in Chapter 5 and student-led learning in Chapter 6.

Overview of the Three Components

Keeping **teacher voice** in the forefront of learning and leadership is a critical success factor for an innovative professional learning process. This means encouraging teachers to express their dreams and ideas with confidence and conviction. Paying close attention to what our valued practitioners say is always important! Yet somewhere in our collective professional history, teachers across the country have begun to quietly retreat to their own isolated classrooms, and their perspectives regarding how and when students learn best are lost to annual accountability data and standardized instruction. Therefore, our Transform Academy's driving question, "What does it mean when we say we want our students to be future ready?" could only be answered through the combined voices, thoughts, and power of all of our teachers.

Openly stating an innovative idea can be precarious in our schools today when the focus seems to be exclusively on tried and true methods to meet accountability standards. So, when it came to risk taking, our academy teachers needed to know they were in a judgment-free setting. This was accomplished in two ways. First, teachers knew they had been selected by their principal for this work, so from the beginning they felt supported by their campus leaders. Second, within the safety of the academy environment they felt as though they had **open permission to dream.** This meant they could verbalize new ideas, try different techniques, redesign classrooms, and make curriculum adjustments in a setting where visioning and dreaming were relished. As teachers learned about new ideas through research, field trips, and exchanges with their Transform Academy colleagues, they began to say things such as, "What if we adjust the sequence of the science curriculum to match our mathematics classes or try to use more project-based learning in language arts?" They welcomed the response given by the academy facilitators and campus leaders, "Let's write a plan and see what happens." (In Chapter 4, we will examine in greater depth how open permission to dream leads to transformational learning.)

Differentiated innovative ideas began to surface as academy participants connected research findings and instructional practices. It is here that we witnessed participants planning a variety of student-centered transformations based on their research and experience. Two of these differentiated innovative ideas were creating flexible classroom environments and encouraging students to lead their own learning experiences. During this time, our participants shared, "We think it is time to ask the students about what they think would improve school." Students responded without hesitation, providing feedback that included working in groups more often, using technology, making learning relevant to their worlds, and changing the way they are assessed. This led to investigations into new types of furniture, ways to maximize student engagement through digital tools, and project-based learning. Throughout the academy we worked to keep abundant, exciting, and innovative ways to engage all students within our participants' reach. We did this by supporting their ideas and providing assistance with research and policy navigation. The academy participants commented, "As we undertake differentiation for student learning needs, we learn the importance of innovation." (In Chapters 5 and 6, we will study differentiated innovative ideas by looking at how teachers implemented flexible learning environments and student-led learning, respectively.)

As an academy year progresses, emerging visions are fueled by these components. First, teacher voice is empowered by collaborative innovation and leadership. Then, open permission to dream is encouraged by reaching for new methods for teaching and learning. Finally, supporting differentiated innovative ideas leads to understanding the positive influences of student-centered classrooms. Let's begin with a deeper examination of how teacher voice is affected by leadership opportunities and a collaborative innovator mindset.

Inspiring Teacher Voice

As the second month of the academy began, participants increasingly relied on the supportive aspects of their learning cultures and the voices of a diverse group of determined teachers to bring forward innovative leadership. Learning about the strengths of the other participants and ways to interact with peer teacher leaders led to the individual and collective expression of teacher voice and to innovative strategies to improve student participation in their own learning. Understanding Figure 1.1 Framework for Transforming a Learning Culture was essential for the participants to be comfortable when sharing their dreams and developing mutual trust when taking risks.

Figure 3.2 shows teacher voice as the first key component of an emerging vision. In this component, teacher leadership and collaborative innovator mindsets interact to strengthen and support the way teachers express their ideas, influence innovative thinking, and inspire student engagement. We will examine teacher leadership first.

Figure 3.2 Excerpt From Emerging Vision: Teacher Voice

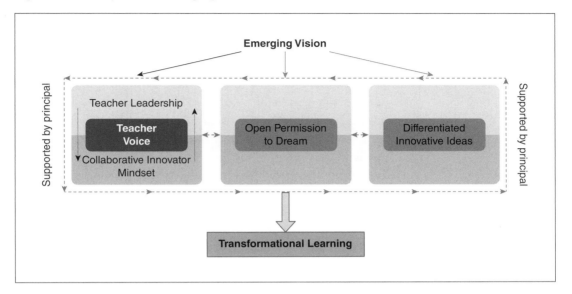

Teacher Leadership

With the start of Session 2, the academy teachers settled into research-ing innovative strategies to increase teacher collaboration and student engagement. They studied a variety of sources and shared information so that everyone heard the new and exciting strategies they discovered in their research reviews. Along with juried journal research, they included information from content and method experts. Findings and ideas were also gathered from videos, books, magazine articles, blogs, social media (Twitter, Pinterest), community members, and professional associations. For example, teachers read the writings of thought leaders in school transformation, then followed these leaders on Twitter and sought out the professional conferences where these educational giants were scheduled as speakers. Academy participants combined efforts and made Pinterest boards to display creative ideas for innovative learning environments. The lively boards included colorful furnishings made with found objects and the latest in manu-factured flexible classroom furniture. These new ways to research and communicate provided practice, feedback, and validation for newly forming collaborative leadership roles.

Further, our instructional leaders continuously searched for the best methods to encourage student engagement while learning. This meant increasing their own capacity to create educational experiences that sparked students' imaginations and changed their attitudes about what it means to go to school each day. Our energized Transform Academy teacher-leaders pointed out that in order to bring about change, they needed to experiment with innovative lesson plans, instructional methods, curriculum sequencing, and adapting learning environments to naturally increase student engagement. For example, as they shared how to use online portfolios for student-led parent conferences, the team honestly discussed both successes and areas needing improvement. This gave them an opportunity to support and encourage one another through frank conversations about growing their craft and moving others to understand the value of their work. With these thoughts, we were beginning to see the development of a new emerging vision with teachers leading the way both in the academy and on their campuses.

As encouraging teacher leadership becomes a transformation objective, the collaborative innovator emerges. Building upon having their voices heard and being given leadership opportunities in collaborative groups during the academy and on their campuses, our participants began to develop positive leadership attributes such as relying on a strong research base for decisions and communicating ideas clearly to a team while considering the perspectives of others. Further, they embraced creative thinking as a way to envision and mind the future. In the next section, we will explore the ways mindsets influence teacher voice.

Time to Collaborate!

Now is a good time to complete **Activity 3.1 Compass Points** and **Activity 3.2 Building a Tower,** found at the end of this chapter.

Collaborative Innovator Mindset

The collaborative innovator mindset is the second element inspiring teacher voice in an emerging vision. As an educator's ways of thinking about creative possibilities for student learning experiences develop, his thinking begins to resemble that of an innovator (Couros, 2015). An innovator is someone who does things differently for a reason. As educators, we sometimes think that we know everything we need to know or that we have learned all there is to know. We believe there is no reason to do anything differently. Teachers often express the thought, "My way has always worked in the past. Just look at my results." Unfortunately, teacher practices then become stagnant and teachers lack the motivation to change as students, technology, and the world change around them. Typically, resistance to change occurs when we keep ourselves isolated (Marzano, Hefflebower, Hoegh, Warrick, & Grift, 2016).

When teachers are part of a collaborative team it is difficult to stay professionally stagnant. A collaborative team of teacher leaders naturally wants to grow and learn and inspire others to grow along with them. When a teacher grows an innovator's mindset, the collaborative environment builds capacity as well. Collaborative innovators question their colleagues and ask for more; they expand their thinking with others to read and listen to experts and students; they go outside of their classroom and school to see how others are changing their learning environment; and they are open to trying a new way, knowing it may not be totally perfect in the outcome. In short, they are explorers who are never satisfied with the status quo. Innovation and collaboration can force educators out of their comfort zones and encourage them to explore the possibilities that can come from new and different ways of thinking. Growth emerges from the stagnation of isolation when teachers are supported in their collaborative innovation, encouraged as leaders, and have built trust within their team. Through their collective leadership, teachers contribute to revitalizing learning cultures in their schools and communities.

Time to Collaborate!

Now is a good time to complete **Activity 3.3 The Power of Yet**, found at the end of this chapter.

How Mindsets Influence Teacher Voice

When we first introduced Figure 2.1 Voices of Teachers Growing Toward Collaborative Innovation in Chapter 2, we described how educational transformation moves from a standardized or status quo way of thinking to increasingly more innovative approaches. Further, innovation is expanded when teachers remove themselves from an isolated environment and begin to productively collaborate, intentionally plan, and study with other educators. This collaboration may occur in a variety of ways: in their own or a neighboring school, during higher education coursework or professional development, and even on social media. As we experienced our teachers reaching collaborative innovator mindsets, we also saw that the Transform Academy process resulted in shifts in teacher beliefs about their own abilities and those of their students.

According to Carol Dweck (2006), a mindset is one's beliefs about basic traits such as talents, intelligence, and personality. People generally fall into one of two types of mindsets: fixed or growth. Within a fixed mindset, people think that traits such as intelligence and talent are set and immoveable. While they readily assess and document these traits, they do not feel they can be changed. To a person with a fixed mindset, if one does not have a natural talent to accomplish a goal then the dream will never materialize. You may hear a teacher say, "I got the slow class this year and there is nothing I can do to help these kids. They keep saying everything is too hard. They have always been unmotivated and slow and always will be." The students believe they cannot grow, and sadly, their teacher feels he is not capable of teaching them. Thus, both the teacher and his students have fixed mindsets.

A growth mindset is quite different. With this mindset, people believe that basic traits can be developed and improved with hard work and effort. Teachers with a growth mindset are undeterred in the face of challenges when it comes to student success. This is the teacher who says, "Bring me any student and I will help her find her talents, gifts, and strengths. We will use everything possible to increase her achievements, and this student will leave my class with a love of learning and the determination to succeed in any endeavor." This teacher has a growth mindset and so will her students.

As the Transform Academy teacher-participants spent time learning about mindsets, they found that they could not afford to have a fixed mindset if they were to assist students with preparing for the future. They increasingly came to believe that as a collaborative team they could move any and all students forward. Over the year, our teachers' beliefs grew unquestionably into growth mindsets. After really listening to student voice, teachers found that students were capable of setting learning goals and designing ways to demonstrate their personal learning outcomes. In turn, these student-set learning outcomes provided both extended and deeper learning. For example, teacher expectations were exceeded by student goals during a project to create a new sport. Students went beyond naming the sport, giving it scoring rules, and uniforms to determining where the sport would be played during different climates, national league creation, and Olympic trials. In their efforts to create innovative instructional practices, teachers moved from isolation to collaboration as well as from standardization to innovation as they shared ways to bypass one size fits all schooling.

Considering Figure 2.1 Voices of Teachers Growing Toward Collaborative Innovation, it is possible to envision the teachers at the top of the chart as having a growth mindset and those on the bottom as holding a fixed mindset. The following discussion and Figure 3.3 demonstrate how this may occur in a transforming learning culture.

Figure 3.3 Teacher Mindsets in a Transforming Learning Culture

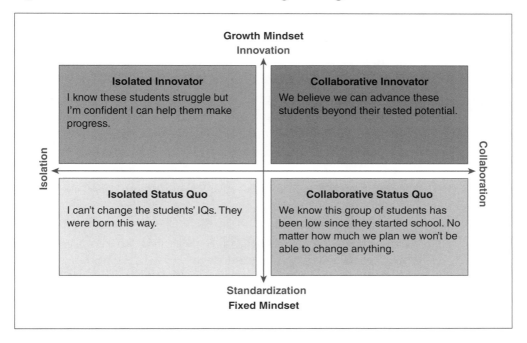

Teachers included in both the isolated status quo and collaborative status quo quadrants have a fixed mindset. They are focused on the way school has always been and the permanence of a student's ranking based upon tests and prior achievement. A teacher in the collaborative status quo has begun the process of collaboration with others but still does not wish to make changes based upon the new ideas or educational research. A teacher who is considered to be collaborative status quo will most likely not be in this phase for long. He or she has become part of a group effort that ultimately leads to innovative thinking through the support of leadership and teamwork.

In addition, there are educators who work and research in isolation to develop innovative methods to enhance their learning environments. They believe they can improve student achievement through their own determination. Unfortunately, they do not share much of what they learned with their colleagues. They are isolated innovators with a growth mindset who rely solely on their own abilities to promote student success.

The ultimate destination for transformational thinking is to be part of the collaborative innovator quadrant. These teachers see beyond any challenges to student success because they have a growth mindset. They also know the power of a collaborative team and believe this support will aid them in reaching all students. This team is willing to do whatever it takes to provide a successful learning experience for *all* students.

The emerging vision of a learning culture is driven by a group of teachers who could at one time or another be a part of any of the quadrants. The ultimate goal is to move as many teachers as possible toward the collaborative innovator quadrant. One principal noted that it would be very difficult to have a faculty consisting entirely of one of the quadrants because as a profession, teachers are always growing. Principals leading a transformation process systematically increase teacher voice through collaborative leadership and decision-making opportunities. Further, they maintain and model a growth mindset as they support the efforts of their teachers. The pinnacle for teacher voice is a teacher leader whose collaborative innovator mindset fosters growth for all students. The most important things a principal can do at this time is provide support and then allow the teachers to take the lead in revitalizing the learning culture of the school.

At the start of a Transform Academy, teachers need to find their own voices in this new professional learning setting. Next, they need to identify and understand the differing voices around them. To do this we used Activity 3.1 Compass Points, Activity 3.2 Building a Tower, and Activity 3.3 Power of Yet. When an appreciation of an individual's unique contribution develops, then all voices are heard and appreciated as the Transform Academy team is strengthened. For example, teachers find that there are other members who think like they do (knowing technology is important, following the curriculum standards), but then other teachers have a different point of view (wanting more digital devices, would like more freedom to choose the curriculum standards to teach), which causes vigorous team discussions. Just as in their campus PLCs, there are academy teachers with strengths in organization and out of the box thinking, while others contemplate new ideas first and then foster group participation. This leads to powerful teacher leadership and collaborative innovator mindsets. A learning culture that encourages and celebrates every teacher's unique voice is essential for dreaming, innovation, and transformation.

Professional Learning for Transform Academy Session 2

If we were truly going to empower teacher voice in this process, we knew that each Transform Academy session should focus on learning experiences that would challenge teachers' current thinking and practices. We needed them to step outside of their comfort zones and, in the process, shift their thinking. As we reflected on Session 1, we were quite certain that participants had walked out that day wondering whether they would ever get comfortable with being uncomfortable.

But we also knew that they were excited and passionate about transforming the way teaching and learning looked in their classrooms. With that in mind, we felt confident we could provide the support they needed to make the transformation happen.

Developing Teacher Voice

Using the feedback from Session 1 along with our Transform Academy project design, the facilitation team developed a plan for Session 2 that would be an action-packed day of learning. It included activities to help participants learn more about one another and group dynamics. It also included opportunities for them to experience innovation and creativity. We planned activities that would allow time for reflecting on their mindsets while determining the link between their own mindsets and the visioning document. More important, we wanted them to think about ways they could apply this learning to their practices in the classroom.

Since the participants included elementary, intermediate, and high school teachers from a variety of grade levels and content areas, we thought it was quite possible that many of them had never had long-term contact with teachers other than those in their buildings or content areas. We began this day with the intent of helping the teachers get to know one another better. We also wanted them to understand how they approach and engage in group work. This year of learning was going to involve multiple opportunities for group work, and we needed that work to be as productive as possible.

Compass Points

Activity 3.1 Compass Points allowed us to involve the teachers in some self-reflection regarding how they approach and engage in group work. As the facilitator explained the characteristics of group members at each compass point, people automatically began to determine which compass point best fit them. They moved into their compass point groups and began responding to the questions on the handout. Based on the level of noise in the room we knew they were actively engaged in this activity. After each grouped shared their responses we debriefed the activity. We heard comments such as, "I've always been frustrated with one of my teammates who can't ever seem to make a decision. She always wants to think about all of the eventualities before starting to work, while I like to begin quickly and get a project going." We also heard comments like, "She's a North (likes to jump in and start to work). No wonder I always have to be the one to question whether we really have a viable plan in place before we leap into something!"

The teachers learned so much about one another in this activity. They found that being aware of how others work helps groups function more productively. In addition, they learned how their personal "direction" impacts others in the group. Most important, they learned the strengths associated with each direction so they could perform at optimum levels in their group work. This type of performance would be essential throughout this year of transformation, and we needed to bring an awareness to it as we began communicating, collaborating, problem solving, and creating in this new professional learning community.

Building a Tower Challenge

Once the teachers had a better understanding of how they approach and engage in group work, we needed to involve the participants in an activity that would allow them to experience the dynamics of teamwork and collaboration. The activity would give us time to observe them in action, allowing us to get to know our learners better. The activity would also prime them to begin thinking about innovation and creativity in a new way, outside of the regular instructional sense. Completing Activity 3.2 Building a Tower would allow us to accomplish those goals.

We asked the participants to form teams of four, making sure they did not stay in a group with someone from their own campus. Once the facilitator provided the goals and the rules for completing the challenge, the fun began. Watching a roomful of teachers work through this activity was something to behold. Initially there was a low murmur in the room, each team quietly developing their plan for creating the structure. You could tell the competitive nature of some of the teams and they were not sharing their secrets. As time passed, the room filled with varying levels of conversation, laughter, and lots of sighs. During the activity, the facilitators walked around the room providing feedback to the teams and keeping the entire group informed about the progress of various groups.

When the timer went off, signifying the end of the 18 minutes allocated for the activity, there were various reactions from the group. We heard comments that ranged from "No, we're not ready yet!" to

"Finally! This was so frustrating!" We measured the freestanding structures that several teams constructed and determined the tallest of those structures. The winning team shared their strategy for successfully completing the challenge. We were once again reminded of the behaviors of the four "directions" during group work.

The Power of Yet

The thoughts shared in the discussion following Activity 3.2 Building a Tower were the perfect segue into Activity 3.3 Power of Yet. As the facilitator posed the initial questions to the group, it was clear that building a freestanding structure was difficult for some and a welcome challenge for others. Once we viewed a video featuring Carol Dweck, they could identify with a fixed or growth mindset regarding the challenge.

Given that this activity was developed as a blended learning experience, we led them to the content we had created in the learning management system. After reviewing the assignment, we left the learning to them. They found comfortable areas to complete their independent work and began reading articles about fixed and growth mindsets. After reading the articles they worked in their table groups to create a product (on a piece of chart paper) that reflected their learning.

Once the charts were mounted on the walls around the room, the participants completed a gallery walk that allowed them to confirm their understanding of fixed and growth mindsets as well as stimulate new thinking. Each group took a picture of their completed chart and uploaded it into the learning management system. This would be a record of their thinking that could be revisited later.

Since the visioning document (TASA, 2008) supports innovative thinking and practices in the classroom and might possibly require a growth mindset to implement, we included it as part of the activity. The participants were directed to work with colleagues from their own campus. Using the visioning document, they needed to consider the following questions:

1. Which one of the five articles may become the focus of my personal learning plan and transformation target this year in Transform Academy?

2. Which of the premises in that article do I care deeply about and want to implement in my classroom?

As we walked around the room and listened to the conversations, we could tell they were making decisions about the premises they wanted to study and implement in their classrooms. Using a digital spreadsheet, the participants inserted information regarding the article and premise(s) that might be the focus of their work for the year. This information would assist us in determining groups and providing appropriate resources for the next session.

The activity concluded with time for the participants to reflect upon and respond to questions. More specifically, they needed to think about their personal mindsets and how that might impact the implementation of their plans and transformation targets. They also needed to reflect on their understanding of growth mindset. Applying their current understanding to their practices in the classroom as well as determining what else they wanted to learn would be important as they tackled the hard work of transforming teaching and learning in their classrooms.

This had been a thought-provoking activity for the participants. They wrestled with what they wanted to do versus what they thought they could actually accomplish. Each one was in the role of decision maker, responsible for determining the outcome of his or her fate. So much of what we had uncovered during the growth and fixed mindset activity was playing out right in front of them and once again, they were having to get comfortable with being uncomfortable.

Tapping Student Potential: It's Time!

A professional text was the resource for Activity 3.4, the final activity of the day. Since many of the premises within the articles of the visioning document (TASA, 2008) focus on student engagement and motivation, we selected *Who Owns the Learning? Preparing Students for Success in the Digital Age* (November, 2012). In order to build background knowledge about Alan November's work and the book, we viewed the video "Who Owns the Learning? Preparing Students for Success in the Digital Age." As the participants viewed the video, they documented their thinking on a T-chart. The discussions at their table groups following the video were better than we could have imagined. Their "wonders" were not only leading them into the book but taking them back into the visioning document as well.

> # Time to Collaborate!
>
> Now is a good time to complete **Activity 3.4 Designing Student Learning Experiences,** found at the end of this chapter.

Once the facilitator provided an overview of the first chapter, the participants separated into the four assigned groups and began reading and reflecting on the assigned chapter. It was interesting to observe the participants grapple with the ideas as they read and reread the text, seeking clarification.

Since they were to become the "experts" on this chapter, they felt responsible for being able to relay the information accurately. As they discussed the chapters and responded to the questions, we knew they were intrigued by the alternate means of approaching teaching and learning in their classrooms and, at the same time, concerned about losing control of the way students would be learning. After returning to their original groups, each chapter "expert" at the table led the group through the four questions and responses. Just as we expected, there was much excitement about all of the options available for preparing students to be future ready. They began referencing the visioning document (TASA, 2008), noting an alignment between their new learning and the document. More important, they began seeing how they might implement some of the ideas in their own classrooms. As the activity culminated, each participant shared an idea he would implement in the classroom. We were excited about their plans for increasing student engagement and motivation in their classrooms and knew it would be important to revisit this topic in future sessions.

KEY IDEAS

During Session 2, teachers learned to lead transformative thinking in the professional learning process. As a result of increasing teacher voice through leadership and collaborative innovation, new ways to engage students were implemented. Teachers sharing a growth mindset rather than a fixed one transitioned into the role of collaborative innovators as they left their isolated, standardized practices behind.

DISCUSSION QUESTIONS

1. In which areas of your learning culture is teacher voice encouraged?

2. How does collaboration look and sound at your campus?

3. How are you monitoring the effectiveness of collaboration at your campus?

4. As a leader in a culture of collaboration and innovation, how will you guide and support innovators in your school?

ACTIVITY 3.1 COMPASS POINTS

Activity 3.1 is based on an activity developed in the field by educators affiliated with the National School Reform Faculty (NSRF).

NSRF®
National School Reform Faculty®
Harmony Education Center

Compass Points Activity
North, South, East and West:
An exercise in understanding preferences in group work
NSRF, Autumn 2015

Facilitation Difficulty: ⏱ 45-50 min.   In this form, groups up to 25   No preconference

Purpose — To understand a variety of tendencies in group working behaviors. This exercise uses descriptions of preferred actions when working together, helping us to understand how our own and others' tendencies affect our working interactions.

Group size — In this form, groups of 8-25. May be modified for larger or smaller groups.

Preparation — Setup chart paper on each of four walls designating the four points of the compass. Label them: North (Acting), East (Big Picture), South (Caring), and West (Details). Place a second blank piece of chart paper adjacent to each. Bring sufficient copies of the Compass Points Activity Worksheet for all participants.

Options — Compass Points II and Compass Points III.

Steps:

1. **Setup** — (5-7 min.) Review the purpose of the activity, then direct participants to examine the chart below (Figure 1). Read through the descriptions of work styles and elaborate on the behaviors or preferences of each direction. Distribute handouts. Ask participants to think about the behaviors they gravitate towards when they're at work with peers, as opposed to the behaviors they may prefer when they're at home with their families, in classrooms with students, or in other scenarios.

   Figure 1

   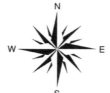

   North: The direction of Action — "Just do it!"
   Motivates and challenges others to get work started or keep it moving, tries new things.

   West: The direction of Detail — wants to know the who, what, when, where, and why before acting. Reliable to get things done, organized.

   East: The direction of the Big Picture — wants to speculate about many possibilities before taking action. Connects individual work with the purpose of organization.

   South: The direction of Caring — wants everyone's feelings to be considered and their voices heard before acting. Communicator, facilitator, negotiator.

2. **Move** — (2 min.) Invite participants to rise from their seats and gather at the chart paper representing the "direction" that they think best describes their group work style. No one "direction" completely describes an individual, but for the sake of this activity, everyone must choose one as their predominant perspective.

3. **Group work** — (10-15 min.) Each smaller group should refer to the Compass Points Activity Worksheet and write their answers to these questions on their chart paper.

   • *What are the strengths of your style?*

Compass Points Activity   page 1 of 2

- *What are the limitations of your style?*

- *What style do you find most difficult to work with and why?*

- *What do people from the other "directions" or styles need to know about you so you can work together effectively?*

- *What do you value about the other three styles?*

- *What catch phrase/symbol/hashtag or mascot would represent your direction and why?*

4. **Report** — (7-10 min.) Ask for a volunteer from one "direction" to report back to the group, referring to their chart paper. Then cycle around the room to hear from each direction.

5. **Debrief** — (10 min.) **It is imperative to debrief this activity,** because reflection and interaction provide essential learning far beyond recognizing one's own "direction."

- *What did you think of the activity? Was it helpful?*

- *What happens if a group is missing a direction?*

- *Note the distribution among the "directions" in your group. What might this distribution mean for how you proceed?*

- *What is the best combination for a group to have? Does it matter?*

- *How can you avoid being driven crazy by people from another "direction"?*

- *How might you use this exercise with others? Students?*

- *When you do an activity like this with students, what might you want to be careful of? (Explore the possibility of stereotyping.)*

- *What body language or other signals might you expect from people of other "directions" when they are impatient with the process? How might they express that they want to move on, based on their "direction" or perspective?*

6. **Optional written silent reflection** —

- *What do you want to remember about this experience?*

- *How might you use it in your work?*

Compass Points Activity   page 2 of 2

National School Reform Faculty®
Harmony Education Center

Compass Points Activity Handout

Use with the Compass Points Activity
NSRF, Spring 2015

Figure 1

North: The direction of Action — "Just do it!"
Motivates and challenges others to get work started or keep it moving, tries new things.

West: The direction of Detail — wants to know the who, what, when, where, and why before acting. Reliable to get things done, organized.

East: The direction of the Big Picture — wants to speculate about many possibilities before taking action. Connects individual work with the purpose of organization.

South: The direction of Caring — wants everyone's feelings to be considered and their voices heard before acting. Communicator, facilitator, negotiator.

Decide which of the four "directions" most closely describes your personal style and gather with others at the chart paper representing that compass point. Then spend 15 minutes answering the following questions as a group and noting your answers on the chart paper.

- *What are the strengths of your style?*

- *What are the limitations of your style?*

- *What style do you find most difficult to work with and why?*

- *What do people from the other "directions" or styles need to know about you so you can work together effectively?*

- *What do you value about the other three styles?*

- *What catch phrase/symbol/hashtag or mascot would represent your direction and why?*

Compass Points Activity Handout   page 1 of 1

Please visit http://resources.corwin.com/MindingTheFuture to access the online resources for this book.

ACTIVITY 3.2 BUILDING A TOWER

Intended Outcome: To provide an opportunity for participants to experience the dynamics of teamwork and collaboration while being innovative and creative problem solvers.

Preparation: Prior to the session place 20 sticks of spaghetti, 1 yard of string, and 1 standard size marshmallow in a brown paper bag or 8" × 10" manila envelope. (You need 1 bag or envelope for each team of 4 participants.) One yard of masking tape for each group is also needed. The strips should be cut ahead of time and placed on the edge of a table for easy distribution. Scissors need to be available.

Facilitator Note: One intended outcome of this chapter is for the reader to understand the importance of celebrating innovation in the classroom. Prior to the session, it would benefit the facilitator to view the video of Tom Wujec's TED Talk "Build a Tower." A link to the video can be found in Online Resource J. Watching the video will help you begin framing specific questions for discussion and reflection at the end of the challenge.

Facilitation:

1. The facilitator provides the goals and rules for the challenge:

   - The goal is to build the tallest freestanding structure possible using the items in the bag. The bag may not be used to build the structure. The base of the structure must touch the table and the entire marshmallow must be on top of the structure.

   - The team is not required to use all 20 spaghetti sticks, string, and tape. The items may be broken or cut into smaller pieces.

   - Teams will have 18 minutes to complete the challenge. When time runs out, a facilitator will measure the height of each structure that remains standing.

   - The winner is the team with the tallest freestanding structure.

   - Prior to starting the timer, ask participants if they need clarification of the rules of the challenge. The facilitator may need to remind them of the rules during the challenge.

2. Start the timer and begin the activity.

   - The facilitator should walk around the room and comment on the innovative structures being created.

   - Remind teams of the remaining time throughout the 18 minutes.

   - Share progress of the teams with the whole group.

3. When time runs out, ask everyone to sit down so that all teams can view the structures.

   - Measure the structures and announce the heights.

   - Identify the winning team and allow them to share the strategy they used to build their structure.

4. View Tom Wujec's "Build a Tower" video and allow time for discussion and reflection. A link to the video can be found in Online Resource J.

The following questions may be used to guide the discussion:

- Was there a leader on your team? How did this make a difference?

- Did anyone on your team seem to be an expert in building a freestanding structure?

- Was everyone actively involved in the building of the structure? Did anyone decide to sit back and watch?

- How did the team respond when the remaining time was announced?

- If you could do this activity again, what actions would you repeat? What would you do differently?

5. After discussing the key lessons learned from this project, provide time for the teams to discuss the implications for collaboration, innovation, and problem solving in their classrooms.

ACTIVITY 3.3 THE POWER OF YET

Intended Outcomes: To introduce participants to the concept of fixed and growth mindsets in order to use that thinking as they take a closer look at the visioning document (TASA, 2008) to narrow the focus of their study.

Preparation: laptops, chart paper, markers, crayons. Facilitator needs to research current professional articles on fixed and growth mindsets and have those articles available in a learning management system.

Facilitator Note: We developed this activity in a learning management system. Not only did it provide an opportunity for the participants to become acquainted with the tool, but it also allowed us to model a blended-learning environment for the participants that allowed flexibility for the learners.

Facilitation:

1. The facilitator begins the discussion by presenting the questions below. Once the participants respond to the questions, the facilitator relates their responses to the concept of fixed vs. growth mindset.

- What did you learn about yourself from participating in Activity 3.2 Building a Tower challenge? Did that surprise you?

- What did you notice about the comments being shared throughout this collaborative activity?

- How did the comments impact your participation in the activity? What were you thinking?

- What impact did the comments have on the success of your collaborative work as a team?

- If your team was not able to create the freestanding structure in 18 minutes, think about this: Are you not smart enough to create it or is it that you were not able to create it *yet*?

2. View Carol Dweck's "Developing a Growth Mindset" video (or a similar video) to provide an opportunity for the entire group to gain a basic understanding of fixed and growth mindsets. A link to the video can be found in Online Resource K.

3. Participants access the various articles provided for them related to fixed and growth mindsets and read the articles independently. (Allow 20–30 minutes.)

4. In table groups, the participants identify the characteristics of fixed and growth mindsets. Using the materials available, each table group creates a product that reflects their learning about fixed and growth mindsets. (Allow 20–30 minutes.)

5. The products are displayed around the room and the groups complete a gallery walk to review the contents of the products. As they view the products each group posts two comments on sticky notes using the following stems: *I agree* and *I wonder.*

6. The facilitator directs the participants to partner with colleagues from the same campus. The partners revisit the first five articles of the visioning document (TASA, 2008). As they review the document they should discuss the following:

- Which one of the five articles may become the focus of my personal learning plan and transformation target this year in Transform Academy?

- Within that article, which of the premises do I care deeply about and want to implement in my classroom?

7. The facilitator gathers the group together and provides a digital spreadsheet on which participants insert information regarding the premise that might be the focus of their work for the year.

8. In closing, the facilitator provides time for the participants to reflect and respond in writing to the following questions:

- How might your current mindset impact the implementation of your personal learning plan and transformation target?

- How will your understanding of growth mindset translate to your practices in the classroom?

- What do you need to know more about in order to be successful with the implementation in your classroom?

ACTIVITY 3.4 DESIGNING STUDENT LEARNING EXPERIENCES

Intended Outcomes: To introduce participants to one author's ideas for redesigning assignments created for students

Preparation: individual copies of Online Resource L.2

Facilitation:

1. Provide a brief book introduction for *Who Owns the Learning? Preparing Students for Success in the Digital Age,* by Alan November (2012).

2. View Alan November's video, "Who Owns the Learning?" A link to the video can be found in Online Resource L.1. While participants are viewing the video, they should record their thinking on the Online Resource L.2 handout, responding to the prompts *He said* and *I wonder.*

3. In groups at their tables, the participants share the information recorded on their T-charts, allowing time for other group members to reflect and respond.

4. The facilitator summarizes the T-chart conversations, making a connection between the conversations and Chapter 1. The facilitator then provides an overview of Chapter 1.

5. While they are seated at their tables, start numbering participants from one to four, making sure that each table has at least one of each number represented. Then divide the room into four areas and assign each number (1, 2, 3, and 4) an area in the room. The participants should move to the area of the room that matches their assigned number.

6. Once the groups settle in their new areas, assign one of the following chapters to each group: The Student as Tutorial Designer, The Student as Scribe, The Student as Researcher, and The Student as Global Communicator and Collaborator.

   - The members of each group should read the four questions at the end of the assigned chapter prior to reading in order to set the purpose for reading.

   - As they read the chapter, they should indicate areas of the text that relate to the questions.

   - Once they finish reading the chapter they should begin discussing the questions and recording their responses in a format that can be shared when they return to their original table groups.

7. Once the groups have completed this task the facilitator should pull the group together again, asking them to return to their original table groups.

8. Once all participants are settled at their tables the facilitator provides information related to the next series of tasks.

   - The person with the information from Chapter 2 begins by reviewing the responses to each of the four questions from the chapter, allowing time for reflection and further discussion. (It may be best to set a timer for 10 minutes for the review of each chapter.)

   - Once the review of Chapter 2 is finished, the person with Chapter 3 begins reviewing the responses to each of the four questions from the chapter, followed by Chapter 4 and then Chapter 5.

9. The facilitator provides the group with a final question for the day: What one idea did you learn today that you will take back to your classroom and implement this month?

   - After giving the participants a few minutes to reflect on the question, the facilitator directs the participants to make a big circle, standing shoulder-to-shoulder and facing the center of the circle.

   - The facilitator begins the activity by sharing a comment by Alan November. In the video, November suggests, "Maybe the real work isn't learning about technology but redesigning the assignments we give kids."

   - The facilitator selects the person to his or her right to quickly share his or her response to the question.

   - The person to the right of that person shares next. This procedure continues around the circle until all participants have shared their ideas.

   - The facilitator shares a final comment from Alan November's book: "Our approach to education must evolve along with its tools, processes, and outcomes. We are already experiencing a cultural shift toward collaboration and learning empowerment in U.S. schools, as we realize that we must go beyond testing to have students demonstrate that they own their learning experiences and can apply the knowledge they have learned" (2012, p. 24).

   - The facilitator thanks the participants for their thoughtful responses and reminds them that they will be asked to share the progress on the implementation of their ideas in our next session.

Suggested Action Items

Action Items	Progress Checks			
1. Review steps taken from the last chapter. Make planning adjustments and communication updates as needed.	☐ Not started	☐ In progress	☐ Completed	☐ NA
2. Prioritize your needs and complete the professional learning activities in this chapter.				
• Activity 3.1 Compass Points	☐ Not started	☐ In progress	☐ Completed	☐ NA
• Activity 3.2 Building a Tower	☐ Not started	☐ In progress	☐ Completed	☐ NA
• Activity 3.3 The Power of Yet	☐ Not started	☐ In progress	☐ Completed	☐ NA
• Activity 3.4 Designing Student Learning Experiences	☐ Not started	☐ In progress	☐ Completed	☐ NA
3. Review calendars for study, meeting, journaling, data checks, and communicating results.	☐ Not started	☐ In progress	☐ Completed	☐ NA

CHAPTER 4

Open Permission to Dream

Sessions 3–6

The future belongs to a very different kind of person with a very different kind of mind—creators and empathizers, pattern recognizers and meaning makers.

—DANIEL PINK

Getting Acquainted With This Chapter

Educators typically enter the classroom with their experiences as a student themselves, ideas from student teaching, and their passion for learning. They may not always realize that society has a huge expectation that they will change the world one student at a time. The Transform Academy experience reminds teachers to value their professional learning opportunities, to take risks to make learning more engaging for students, and that the world is constantly changing around the school building. This chapter emphasizes the importance of consistent research and renewal of the adult learning process for the sake of the students who are preparing for a very different future.

If Only We Could . . .

Why would anyone decide to become a teacher? Most educators would wholeheartedly answer that they want "to make a difference in the lives of students and prepare them for the future." If quizzed further, they may say that they had a favorite teacher who influenced them because he or she made learning fun or interesting. This special teacher may have even shared a little about his or her own life or passions for a subject that hit a chord. Then comes the energetic statement, "And I want to teach the same way Mr. X (or Ms. Y) did!" This tells us that as teachers enter the profession, their expectations of what their daily work will be like are sometimes set by their personal school experiences. Similarly, you may have heard a non-educator say that he knows all about school because he went to one. And despite our lengthy educations in instruction and curriculum methods, we may at times do the same thing—teach the way we were taught. If we are not careful, our beliefs about schooling can be set by our own experiences and biases. Another viewpoint belongs to the teacher who begins her career using the best methods of the day and then never adjusts or changes. This is the person who says, "I have taught this way for 20 years and have been successful in the delivery of my content. This works so well I am continuing this way until I retire." Early in her teaching career, a teacher we know returned to the classroom of one of her own grade school teachers to observe a lesson. As she expectantly sat in the back of the familiar classroom, her teacher walked up and handed her a worksheet with the following comment, "Does this look familiar? It is the same worksheet you did when you were in my class! It is a difficult one; my classes always have a hard time with this." Fourteen years later, students were doing the same worksheets in the same order, having the same problems, year after year. Sadly, there was no change or innovative thought in sight.

This is why continuous professional learning that includes a plan for intentional learning and improvement is so important. The more our Transform Academy teachers discovered about the requirements of today's learners, the more they realized that they needed to reflect on their philosophy of being an educator. If they sincerely wanted to make a difference in the lives of students, then they had to act upon the educational research base by taking a focused look at their instructional practices. This honest assessment would allow them to determine whether they were actually preparing students for the future or simply perpetuating the status quo.

As teachers began to experience a shift in their thinking about teaching and learning, they also developed a new boldness to take risks and mind the future. As they looked around their classrooms, they began to ask some simple questions: Would we want our own child in our classrooms? What kind of learning environment and experiences will engage all students? Will our ideas really work?

Opening the Doors to Dreaming

Session 1 of Transform Academy started with a question and a challenge: "Do you ever wake up in the middle of the night and think, 'I have a great idea to help kids, if only the principal or central administration would let me'? Well, now is your chance!" While everyone was excited to receive open permission to dream, they were also wary of how taking risks would impact student learning. Risk taking without research and planning would not serve students well. Teachers wanted research to validate their dreams, and they needed a plan to develop, monitor, and evaluate their results. Research came in several forms, including books, conferences, webinars, expert addresses, and field trips to learning and business environments. As teachers created ways to make their emerging visions a classroom reality, developing personal learning plans gave them actionable steps for documenting, evaluating, and showcasing their dreams.

Research and Risk Taking

The second key component of an Emerging Vision is *open permission to dream* (see Figure 4.1). In this chapter, we will explore how **research** and **risk taking** inspired the ways our academy teachers transformed their instructional environments and practices in order to foster the innovative learning skills needed for the future. Further, we will present how these ideas were captured in their personal learning plans.

Figure 4.1 Excerpt From Framework for Transforming a Learning Culture: Open Permission to Dream

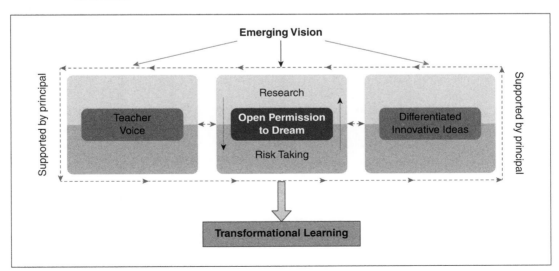

Field Trips, Conferences, and Experts

As our teachers moved toward a collaborative innovator mindset where collaboration is expected and valued, enthusiastic discussions began about the importance of student-centered learning. Their research in the development of future-ready learning experiences and environments demonstrated that today's educators must prepare students to tackle new, or not yet conceived, educational endeavors and careers. Our academy participants discerned that innovative ways to work and learn were increasingly on the horizon, yet imagining the future outside of a traditional school was daunting. Many of our teachers had spent their lives in school. They usually grew up as first-class students followed by employment in education. And as they considered the workforce of the future, they realized they had little experience with the structure of diverse learning or work environments.

Within the Transform Academy, our teachers were knowingly practicing future-ready competencies in their professional learning communities, including interpersonal, metacognitive, and social skills involving communication, collaboration, and problem solving. It was becoming apparent that students would also require opportunities to experience these skills and how they would appear both in the classroom and the workplace. There was an urgent reason to get out of the four walls of the classroom and learn about the experiences to come for students. The group decided it was time to explore classrooms in other schools to learn how their teachers approached 21st-century learning and then visit some professional settings in the community to observe how these skills were applied.

As with most direct learning experiences, our field trips were pivotal. Our teachers were inspired with new information about how stimulating, creative, and collaborative environments could be translated to the classroom. First we visited other teachers' classrooms, including our high school career and technology classes, to see how they engaged learners as problem solvers. Next, we sought out businesses who are impacting the way we live and work today, giving our teachers a new perspective of the world ahead for students. (You can learn more about these trips and how to set them up for your own professional learning programs at the end of this chapter.)

Throughout the academy year, our teachers wished to expand and confirm their dreams by hearing from the experts using both multimedia and "live and in person." They read books, watched videos, and went to conferences to find expert advice on how to design future-ready learning experiences and classroom environments. Further, we introduced district professionals with multifaceted knowledge and skills in fine arts integration and educating gifted students, English language learners, and students with special needs. These district experts showed our teachers how different types of learners approach a variety of learning experiences and how to consider each student's needs as they dreamed. The research and professional learning they asked for and received began culminating in a collective necessity to take a risk and travel down a road that had not been traveled by enough teachers. Their students' futures were at stake, and the way they approached their learners needed to change!

Research and willingness to take risks gave our teachers perspectives into a world that required additional skills beyond the learning standards they were already implementing. These skills would be needed to meet the requirements of a highly global, multidimensional, and connected workforce. To succeed, our students would need to demonstrate their ability to communicate clearly, interact collaboratively, think critically, and create productively. Further, these 21st-century skills had to be integrated throughout the curriculum for the future- and career-ready student. Clarifying these skills would be the next step.

Implementing New Learning Standards

We began this book with some questions. First, "If you want to go beyond standards and accountability, then where are you going?" Second, "What skills do students need to be future ready?" And finally, "Are there changes or additions that can be made in curriculum standards and learning environments to increase student success in school and in their work lives?" Our teachers found good answers, research-based solutions, and practical advice when they decided to study the *Framework for 21st Century Learning*, (Partnership for 21st Century Learning, 2015). The framework illustrates the "21st century learning outcomes" students need to be successful in life along with the support systems required to achieve these outcomes. Of the four support systems presented, our teachers found the "learning and innovation skills" known as the 4Cs to be of special interest to them. The 4Cs standards are considered to be essential for career success as businesses become increasingly global and creative solutions are highly prized. These standards are **critical thinking**, **communication**, **collaboration**, and **creativity.**

During their field trips, our teachers witnessed the 4Cs in action in both classrooms and businesses. As they observed, they found that engaging ways to integrate these learning and innovation standards into existing curricula would be beneficial for students because the standards introduce the skills needed for interactive learning using knowledge gathering, extension, and application to solve a problem or create something new. Additionally, the standards develop students into collaborative leaders and creative thinkers who understand how to communicate and appreciate multiple perspectives. Below we will review these standards as defined by the research and how our Transform Academy teachers began putting the 4Cs into practice.

Critical Thinking and Problem Solving

One of the first areas sparking interest with the Transform Academy was critical thinking and problem solving. This standard includes the systems thinking required to analyze a problem, gather and interpret information, develop ideas, evaluate both potential and actual outcomes, make realistic decisions, and communicate solutions. This type of thinking is seen as students tackle many subject areas including science, mathematics, humanities, and even social problems. The problem situations may invoke the need for knowledge in one or all of these areas. Our academy teachers introduced the critical thinking and problem solving standard when they began teaching students to code a computer program. When a student learns to persist through a problem while coding, then she also learns to apply this thinking to other types of problems. Trial and error are not cumbersome. Recognizing patterns and working through possible solutions become ways for finding innovative pathways.

Communication

In the age of globalization, social media, and the instant transmission of information from one person or group to possibly millions, communication is a vital skill for the future. Further, communication is not necessarily verbal as multimedia messages fly across the globe in seconds. For this standard, students must learn to share information while expressing their thoughts and opinions and, at the same time, acknowledge and understand the perspectives of others. This requires the ability to fully listen and to respond to the ideas of others, whether they are expressed in person, on the Internet, or on social media. Writing appropriate emails, presenting a virtual resume, and maintaining a positive online presence are important skills in this standard.

Collaboration

The industrial model of education was quickly diminishing, and the innovators of the Transform Academy were moving into the future. As with any new type of thinking, sharing ideas and working with others is a key factor for success. Thus, the third C is collaboration. Our teachers were quickly realizing through their own PLCs that collaboration is as important to student achievement as it is to professional success. If students were to learn to work together to accomplish a goal, then insisting that students sit silently in rows, work alone, and cover their work no longer made sense. Teaching the skill of collaboration is closely related to communication and requires flexibility and responsibility. To ensure that students knew how to collaborate, our teachers took three steps. First, they set up learning areas and seating arrangements to encourage collaborative learning. Next they used direct instruction, to teach students how to set norms that outlined conduct standards to respect for team members, resolve conflicts through compromise and empathy, and manage time and responsibilities for task completion when working in groups. Third, students were given time to practice these skills and receive feedback through application. Just as our teachers learned about team building using Activity 3.2 Building a Tower Challenge (see Chapter 3), students were given the opportunity to practice how they collaborated with others to complete a task. To allow students to experience the global workplace, our teachers explored how students in different schools or different instructional periods could collaborate on projects virtually.

Creativity

The fourth C to enter the future-ready learning standards is creativity. This learning and innovation skill encompasses brainstorming new ideas or refining existing ones to create actions or products to benefit students' school, neighborhood, country, or the global community. Like the other innovation and learning proficiencies, creativity depends on its partner skills.

Whether creativity is demonstrated by designing a new type of vehicle, writing a piece of music, photographing nature, or performing in a play, students must integrate both content knowledge and interpersonal skills to conceive and produce their visions. To brainstorm ideas, students need to be responsive to the thoughts of others and honor their perspectives, both while working on a team and reviewing the research of others. Further, they must be ready to use content knowledge to intentionally turn their innovations, dreams, and aspirations into reality.

Our academy teachers saw an interesting student innovation when they posed a problem to their students regarding the need for reteaching concepts to students whose first languages were other than English. A seventh grader proposed that students who demonstrated mastery of a concept should do the reteaching. Another student added that if this reteaching could be done using their technology devices, then the presentation could be saved and reused. The group then concluded that the lessons could be shared across the school for other students and teachers to use. They even thought that parents would like to use the lessons when they were helping their children at home. When creativity is encouraged and ideas are embraced, students excel and the community wins!

To summarize the 4Cs, let's consider Figure 2.1 Voices of Teachers Growing Toward Collaborative Innovation (see Chapter 2) and Figure 3.3 Teacher Mindsets in a Transforming Learning Culture (see Chapter 3) from the perspective of how the teachers in each quadrant would teach these learning and innovation skills. First, to the bottom quadrants we can add the descriptor **Teacher Directed** and to the top quadrants we add **Teacher Facilitated**. Along the horizontal axis we add a student perspective, which moves from **Isolated Student Learning** to **Student Learning Communities**. A teacher in the bottom quadrants maintains the status quo, teaches only the required standards, does not deviate beyond the curriculum, and presents a fixed mindset. The teachers in the top quadrant are innovators and creative in their instructional approaches, including having a growth mindset.

Considering each quadrant individually, you can see that students in the **Isolated/Status Quo/Teacher Directed** quadrant would not be likely to have any exposure to the 4Cs. Learning is teacher directed and only mastery of the curriculum is asked. You can almost hear the teacher in this classroom saying, "Stay in your seats and cover your papers." Next to this quadrant are the **Collaborative/Status Quo/ Teacher Directed** teachers. Students here are fortunate to be in a classroom where collaboration and communication are encouraged. They may not, however, have the opportunity to experience many activities that incorporate critical thinking or creativity as their teacher sticks to the standard curriculum and continues to work with a fixed mindset.

The top two quadrants consist of teachers with growth mindsets who work to facilitate learning through innovative practices. The students in the top left quadrant work in isolation and are solitary in their learning. Their teacher who is an **Isolated/Innovator/Teacher Facilitator** believes that all students should be asked to think critically and be creative.

Figure 4.2 How the 4Cs Are Integrated Into a Learning Culture

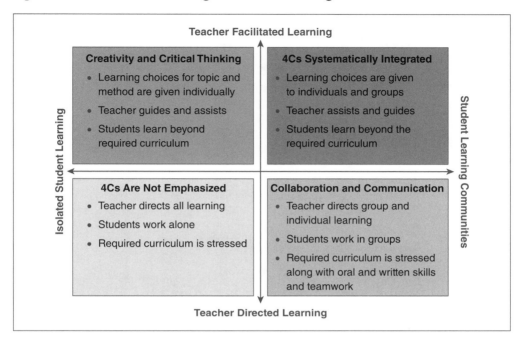

These students have little chance to communicate about their learning with other students or work collaboratively.

The students in the top right quadrant are part of the learning environment facilitated by **Collaborative/Innovator/Teacher Facilitator.** Their daily activities are full of opportunities to learn in collaborative groups while thinking critically, being creative, and communicating their learning in new and innovative ways of their choice (see Figure 4.2).

Coming full circle through the 4Cs, the academy participants felt confident they were expanding students' intentional use of both the curriculum and the 4Cs to develop the leaders, creators, problem solvers, innovators, communicators, and collaborators needed in workplaces of the future. The field trips they took validated this learning. Their visits to other schools and business helped them answer two questions:

- What do we want students to know and be able to do in the 21st century?

- What does the application of these skills look like in the workplace?

It was time to develop personal learning plans to bring these ideas to life in the classroom.

Professional Learning for Transform Academy Sessions 3–6

The sessions described below are the heart of the academy, during which some of the most profound work is accomplished. It is also a time when multiple activities begin as momentum and excitement for collaborative innovation builds. In preparation for this, we recommend allotting ample time for participants to continue to explore, learn, and connect professionally. Across these sessions, academy participants begin to focus their dreams by articulating their goals and developing personal learning plans. Simultaneously, research continues using experts and field trips. All of this takes some planning and flexibility on the part of the academy facilitators!

Personal Learning Plans

Personal Learning Plans (PLPs) serve as a roadmap for academy participants as they begin bringing their dreams to life. The learning plans developed by the academy participants included transformation targets, performance measures, and learning paths. Status updates are also regularly included. The best PLPs provide valuable guidelines for staying on course, documentation of results to validate dreams, and tools for adjusting and reflection. An example of a PLP can be found in Online Resource M. A template is provided in Online Resource N. Remember, these plans will be carried across the remainder of the academy, so have extra professional learning facilitators available as participants write and test their plans.

During previous sessions teachers were asked what they needed to know more about in order to successfully develop and implement their plans for transforming teaching and learning in their classrooms. They provided us with a variety of responses. Some wanted to know more about designing lessons that would allow the locus of control to shift to students. They wanted to know how to shift the responsibility for asking questions from the teacher to the student. Further, they were inspired by Alan November's (2012) work and wanted to look further into the idea of students owning their learning.

The thought of utilizing a project-based learning (PBL) approach in this era of accountability was frightening to some, but they were ready to take the risk and investigate the benefits of PBL. They noticed the alignment of this instructional approach with several articles in the visioning document (TASA, 2008) and believed it would assist them in developing future-ready students. Knowing they had like-minded colleagues to collaborate with in this learning endeavor eased their anxiety. Conversations with their principals provided additional support and comfort as they entered this new territory.

Researching flexible learning environments became an area of interest as well. Many of the participants were not satisfied with the look and feel of their classrooms. They knew they needed a different classroom environment but were not quite sure how to approach and manage changes as they occurred. By focusing their efforts on a flexible learning environment, the participants believed they could have classrooms in which students felt comfortable learning and the learning outcomes would confirm their ideas and research.

As expected, some participants decided they needed to focus their work on the digital environment. They had access to laptops and, in some cases, were already 1:1 with students to laptops in their classrooms. Interactive whiteboards and iPads were available for use at any time. What they had discovered was that today's learners are drawn to technology, but it really was not all about the technology. They had come to realize the *learner* was the key.

The World Outside Our School

Note: The idea of exploring learning environments and field trips in the business workplace occurred throughout the entire timeline of the Transform Academy; however, for the purpose of this book, we have described the "field trips" taken in this chapter. Please refer to the timeline for the entire Academy in Figure I.2 (see Introduction).

The development of PLPs provided us with many options for supporting teachers in their transformation targets as well as the learning path steps included in their plans. Once again, they did not disappoint! As we had expected and planned for in our original draft of the year-long academy, they wanted to go outside the four walls of their classrooms to observe others in their work environments. Although these field trips created some challenges, we knew we had to be true to the intent of the Transform Academy—leading with teacher voice. The phrase "we need a road trip" became a new slogan.

In order to provide this type of support, we scheduled various field trips within the school district as well as in the community. Although this presented a challenge, it was well worth the effort. Transformational learning may not have been possible without these learning experiences.

Classroom Visits

The first field trip involved classroom visits at schools within the district. We contacted principals at campuses that were already implementing new approaches to teaching and learning in some of their classrooms. The rationale and date for the field trip was shared with the principals as well as the specific needs. They were always excited to hear that teachers and central office staff wanted to visit their campuses to observe the early adopters who were already transforming teaching and learning in their classrooms. Not one principal opted out of the visit. They knew the academy was a district initiative and wanted to support it.

Once we had the support of the principals for the site visits, we created a schedule for the day. A template of the schedule can be found in Online Resource O. We wanted the academy teachers to observe as many classrooms in as many schools as possible. Although this was a great idea, it posed its own problems. A member of our facilitation team would need to be available at each campus in order to guide and support the teachers as they completed their observations. We did not want to interrupt the principals in their focused work on the campuses, but they always wanted to be a part of the tour. They were proud of their teachers and students, and this was an opportunity for them to show their support.

Simply providing time to observe a variety classrooms and campuses was not going to result in transformative thinking and learning for our academy teachers. A scaffolded support to connect the visioning document with their observations was needed. Questions were developed to guide their thinking and reflections. As they visited the classrooms they were to focus on these questions:

- *Did you see an example of a teacher as a designer of engaging experiences for students?*
- *Did you see children engaged and learning in a new or surprising way?*
- *In the classrooms that you observed today, is there evidence of a shift in control of learning from the teacher to the student?*
- *What are some ways that you might already be teaching transformatively?*

By focusing their observations and thinking around these four questions, we would have more than enough opportunities for in-depth conversations in the debriefing session in the afternoon.

In order to keep the momentum going throughout the day, the teachers were invited to take a picture in front of each school and tweet something positive about the visit. Each team had a Transform Academy sign they displayed in their picture, and they used the hashtag created for the Transform Academy and the field trip. We were well aware that many teachers, campus and district leaders, school board members, and community members were active on Twitter and would be interested to see this professional learning model in action.

After the teachers completed their site visits, we returned to the training site to debrief the day of learning. Using the Guiding Questions document (see Online Resource R) as the resource for the debriefing activity, the teachers reflected on their day of learning. The final step of the activity focused their attention on the PLPs they had developed. We wanted to make an intentional connection between the classroom visits and their learning plans. This provided another opportunity for them to continue the implementation of the goals in their plans.

Career and Technical Education Classroom Visits

Our driving question for the Transform Academy—What does it mean when we say we want our students to be future ready?—led us to the Career and Technical Education (CTE) classrooms at the high school. These classrooms were ideal for observing some of the real-world skills that were preparing our students for graduation and beyond. As our first step in the planning process, we contacted the district-level CTE administrator.

The district-level CTE administrator supported us through the planning and scheduling of the classroom visits. In her contacts with the campus administrators and the classroom teachers, she shared the reasons for the classroom visits as well as the intended outcomes. Together we developed the schedule for the classroom visits with the intent that these visits would result in an optimal experience for the Transform Academy teachers. District-level personnel from the CTE team as well as the academy facilitators were available to serve as tour guides for each team of teachers.

The week before the field trip, we sent several professional articles to the academy teachers. The articles enabled them to become better acquainted with the 4Cs. On the day of the field trip, each facilitator provided the academy teachers with a copy of Online Resource S.1 for recording their observations. After a quick explanation of the purpose of the observational tool, the facilitators began the classroom tours. Although we had intended for the teachers to be silent observers in the classrooms, that was not the case. They often engaged in conversations and hands-on learning with the students. The students became the teachers.

Once the classroom visits were completed, we returned to the training site and began debriefing the day of learning. As you can imagine, the debriefing session was filled with wonder, purpose, and hope. The elementary school and intermediate school academy teachers were amazed at the level of thinking they witnessed in their former students. The high school academy teachers compared student engagement in learning and the level of thinking in the CTE classrooms with their own classrooms. These reflective practitioners were more committed than ever to transforming teaching and learning in their classrooms.

Visit to an Architect Firm

The first out-of-district field trip was to an architect firm that was in the process of designing the plans for an intermediate school in the district. All it took was one phone call to initiate the plans for a field trip that would result in transformative thinking for all of us. We arranged the first of two planning meetings with three members of their team.

During the initial meeting, we determined the outcomes we were hoping to accomplish. They listened as we shared our expectations:

- To engage with professionals in the real world so that we have a better understanding of what it means to be future ready
- To learn the history of school and classroom space design
- To observe a team at the firm as they engage in their work

Although it was sometimes difficult for us to fully express our ideas about the purpose of the visit, that did not deter the architect team from developing a plan that would accomplish our goals—and more! They expanded upon our ideas and offered new ideas and suggestions. It was apparent that communication, collaboration, critical thinking, and creativity are routine practices for them as they go about accomplishing the tasks involved in their work. That was as real world as it gets.

During the second meeting, the team shared their proposed agenda for the three-hour visit to their office. It far exceeded our expectations and included the following learning opportunities:

- Tour of the office
- Presentation: How architecture interacts with the learning environment

- Presentation: How to hack your classroom—making design a reality for students
- Observation of the team at work

As they shared the details about each item on the agenda, it became clear this was going to be a thought-provoking and highly engaging day for all attendees.

Once we had an agenda for the session, we contacted the principals to extend an invitation to join their teachers on this field trip. The majority of principals accepted the invitation because they believed this would be a great opportunity for them to collaborate and learn with their teachers.

A schedule was developed for two sessions at the firm: Group A in the morning and Group B in the afternoon. Knowing that our group consisted of elementary, intermediate, and high school teachers, we had three different schedules to work around. We developed the schedule to accommodate as many teachers as possible without disrupting their regular work day. A template of the schedule can be found in Online Resource P. Since the sessions at the firm were three-hour sessions, we included a brief schedule for the teachers to follow when they were at the district training site that day. That schedule was listed on the agenda as well. The appropriate schedule was sent to each teacher and principal well in advance, so that if any conflicts existed we could resolve them before the day of the session.

Upon arrival at the firm the teachers were greeted like celebrities. The firm's team took them on a tour of their work areas, allowing time for the teachers to stop, take pictures, and ask questions of the employees. They noticed the firm's core values were proudly displayed along a wall. One teacher commented on the similarities between the firm's core values and the core values at her campus.

Once the tour was completed the teachers were seated in a large conference room. As the team members presented information to the teachers they allowed time for questions and clarification. They also engaged the teachers in a school design activity that not only provided valuable information for the firm but gave the teachers a glimpse into the real work of an architect. That was authentic formative assessment. The session ended with the team modeling a typical design session. The teachers witnessed communication, collaboration, critical thinking, and creativity as the team engaged in their real work. Much to the surprise of the team, the teachers applauded them once they had completed the demonstration. The feedback to the team was just as important as the learning for the teachers.

As expected, this field trip was one of the highlights of the year for the academy teachers. Not only were they able to see beyond the walls of their classrooms and schools but they got to authentically engage with architects in meaningful tasks. It does not get much better than this!

Visit to a Technology Company

The final field trip of the year was truly a road trip. Responding to the requests of the teachers, we scheduled a trip to a technology company. The travel time to the office would be more than two hours and we were not sure if everyone would want to make the trip there and back in one day. In true Transform Academy spirit, they all wanted to attend. Again, we invited the principals to travel with us and, as expected, they accepted.

We contacted the education liaison to arrange for a visit. He was more than willing to work with us on scheduling a date for the tour. Due to the size of our group, he scheduled two times during the day for us to observe and learn. A template of the schedule can be found in Online Resource Q. Our questions for him were simple:

- What does a day in the life of a technology employee look like?
- Why does your company have the reputation for being a great place to work?
- What do our students need to know and do in order to be qualified to work for your company?

Based on these questions, he developed an agenda that began with an orientation followed by a tour of the office. A debriefing session after the tour would allow time for him to respond to questions from the teachers.

On the day of the field trip teachers traveled with their campus team members and principal. Since there was not going to be an opportunity for all of the Transform PLC to be together that day, we decided to use Twitter as our way of connecting with one another. Their assignment for the day included three tweets in response to the following questions:

1. What are you most excited about seeing/learning today?
2. What was the biggest "aha" during the tour?
3. What did you see or hear today that caused you to reflect on your own practices?

While traveling to the office, at least one person from each campus team needed to respond to Question 1. After the tour of the office they would respond to Question 2. Once they returned home, each person would respond to Question 3.

During the orientation session, the guide provided an overview of the history of the company as well as the specific products being developed in this particular location. A tour of the office was next on the agenda. During the tour, he noted the various work areas that were available to the employees. There were individual work-stations with desks, like those we were accustomed to, as well as desks that could be raised and lowered with the push of a button. We walked into mini-conference rooms that were available for an employee to have private phone calls with clients. Areas for eating, resting, and playing could be found in multiple places on the same floor of the office. The tour ended with a debriefing session in a large, light-filled conference room.

As you can imagine, the day was filled with oohs and ahs as well as comments about how learning environments could be more like this work environment. Principals were a captive audience for the Transform Academy teachers that day, and the teachers took full advantage of the situation. Teachers and principals shared their commitments to transforming the learning environments at their campuses and began a new phase in this transformational process.

KEY iDEAS

This chapter reminds us that field trips and learning experiences outside of the classroom can initiate the fulfillment of a student's dreams by opening up new doors for applying learning. Research in many forms can inform the actions teachers implement to improve the learning for themselves and others as they discover the needs of workplace environments. Transform Academy participants found that being given permission to dream and taking risks to influence the learning environment are necessary to increase successful student engagement.

DISCUSSION QUESTIONS

1. What student projects have you imagined or implemented that integrate the new learning standards?

2. Why are research and taking field trips outside the school important for teachers and administrators?

3. How will you and your students know if they are learning the 4Cs?

4. How do we begin student involvement in learning?

Transform Academy Sessions 3-6 Activities

ACTIVITY 4.1 DEBRIEFING CLASSROOM VISITS

Intended Outcome: To provide an opportunity for participants to connect classroom observations with their PLPs

Preparation: Place each question from the Online Resource R on chart paper; place the charts on the wall in four separate areas of the room; make available a different color marker for each chart

Facilitation:

1. The facilitator reviews the four questions on the Guiding Questions document (Online Resource R) with the large group.

2. Participants number off at their tables from 1 to 4. Each number corresponds to one of the four questions on the chart paper. Participants move to the chart that corresponds to their number. Once everyone is at the appropriate chart, each group selects a facilitator for the activity.

3. The facilitator begins by reading the question on the chart and then asks participants to share the information recorded on their Guiding Questions document.

Please visit http://resources.corwin.com/MindingTheFuture to access the online resources for this book.

4. Once everyone in the group has shared his or her reflections, the facilitator asks them to synthesize the information. The facilitator documents their ideas on the chart.

5. After 10 minutes, the large group facilitator signals to the participants that it is time to move clockwise to the next chart and wait for directions. Remind the small group facilitator to take the colored marker as the group moves to the next chart. Each team's responses to the questions will be readily apparent because each team will be responding with a uniquely colored marker.

6. The small group facilitator reads the question on the chart and directs the group to read silently the information on the chart. The group members review the responses on their Guiding Questions document as well.

    a. Place a checkmark next to any items on the chart that someone in the group had written on their Guiding Questions document.

    b. Add ideas to the chart.

    c. Place a star next to any items that members want to learn more about or need clarification about.

7. After 5 minutes, the large group facilitator signals to the participants that it is the time to move clockwise to the next chart and repeat the same process.

8. After the participants return to their tables, the facilitator provides time for them to independently reflect on their learning from the classroom visits. The reflections will be used in the development of their PLPs.

ACTIVITY 4.2 DEBRIEFING CAREER AND TECHNICAL EDUCATION CLASSROOM VISITS

Intended Outcome: To provide an opportunity for participants to connect classroom observations with teaching and learning in their own classrooms

Preparation: The week before the field trip, send each participant links to articles and websites related to the 4Cs. This will give participants an opportunity to reflect on the application of the 4Cs prior to the classroom visits.

Facilitation:

1. The facilitator opens the discussion by asking participants to review their notes on the Observational Tool in Online Resource S.1. As they review they should independently complete the following steps:

    a. Highlight key ideas in your notes.

    b. Select five of the ideas in the highlighted text that caused you to reflect on your own classroom practices.

   c. List the ideas in the "I noticed" column of the Classroom Reflections document in Online Resource S.2.

   d. Reflect on the first idea listed and find an article or premise in the visioning document that aligns to the idea. Document the article and/or premise in the Visioning Document column.

   e. Reflect on the information in the first column again and respond to the prompt in the "I wonder how this might look in my classroom?" column of the chart.

   f. Repeat the process for the next four ideas on the list.

2. In table groups, each teacher shares the three responses to the first idea on his or her chart. When all teachers have shared their first item, they should continue the same process with the remaining items.

3. After everyone has shared the information from his or her chart, the facilitator brings the group back together. The facilitator asks volunteers to share something from the "I wonder how this might look in my classroom?" column.

4. The facilitator challenges the teachers to continue to reflect on their "wonders" and start making the changes in their classrooms.

Suggested Action Items

Action Items	Progress Checks			
1. Review steps taken from the last chapter. Make planning adjustments and communication updates as needed.	☐ Not started	☐ In progress	☐ Completed	☐ NA
2. Form a team to plan teacher field trips including:				
• Sites to visit	☐ Not started	☐ In progress	☐ Completed	☐ NA
• Participant lists	☐ Not started	☐ In progress	☐ Completed	☐ NA
• Host and participant requirements such as permissions for photographs	☐ Not started	☐ In progress	☐ Completed	☐ NA
• Daily schedule	☐ Not started	☐ In progress	☐ Completed	☐ NA
• Participant documentation (virtual and/or paper)	☐ Not started	☐ In progress	☐ Completed	☐ NA
• Debriefing activities	☐ Not started	☐ In progress	☐ Completed	☐ NA
3. Form a team to plan training and support for developing PLPs.				
• Review the resources provided for this chapter	☐ Not started	☐ In progress	☐ Completed	☐ NA
• Schedule technical support for the planning process including writing goals and measures	☐ Not started	☐ In progress	☐ Completed	☐ NA
• Schedule plan reviews and updates until the end of the academy year.	☐ Not started	☐ In progress	☐ Completed	☐ NA
4. Prioritize your needs and complete the professional learning activities in this chapter.				
• Activity 4.1 Debriefing Classroom Visits	☐ Not started	☐ In progress	☐ Completed	☐ NA
• Activity 4.2 Debriefing Career and Technology Visits	☐ Not started	☐ In progress	☐ Completed	☐ NA
5. Review calendars for study, meeting, journaling, data checks, and communicating results.	☐ Not started	☐ In progress	☐ Completed	☐ NA

CHAPTER 5

Flexible Learning Environments

Session 7

The real role of leadership in education . . . is not and should not be command and control. The real role of leadership is climate control—creating a climate of possibility. If you do that, people will rise to it and achieve things that you completely did not anticipate and couldn't have expected.

—SIR KEN ROBINSON

Getting Acquainted With This Chapter

One of the most interesting inventions causing people to think about innovation is a driverless car. Just as a driverless car needs guidance from a passenger, a student still needs guidance from a teacher. As the teacher steps to the side and facilitates while the student leads the learning in a flexible learning environment, transformational journeys begin to occur.

Now Ask the Students

Picture a seventh-grade boy walking confidently across an auditorium stage to greet one of the giants of digital education. The student's mission is to explain why access to technology and working in a student learning community is a better way for the students in his class to learn. The student greets the esteemed presenter with a handshake and a generous, wide smile. Hair coaxed into place, wearing a new tie with a yellow shirt and black jeans, he is eager to share his opinions with the grandfatherly gentleman who is genuinely anticipating this opportunity to interview a 12-year-old digital native. Our expert asks the student to tell his story and steps back to listen. Our young man does not disappoint the interviewer or the audience of more than 75 teachers and administrators attending a three-day digital learning conference. Attendees from across the urban and suburban area eagerly lean forward to hear the wisdom of this engaging crusader for student choice and technology. Using his own PowerPoint presentation, our student articulates what happened when his teacher introduced project-based learning using student learning communities, tablets, interactive whiteboards, and laptops to his class. The description includes how he worked with classmates to solve a scientific problem, their creative ideas to solve the complex problem, and then how it felt to collaborate and present a solution as a team to the class.

Then he continues, "So, what makes learning this way so much better than a worksheet is that when you use a worksheet you can only learn just what is on the worksheet." He holds up his hands to show the audience the limits of an 8½" by 11" sheet of paper. "But when you can use the Internet and research sites, you can learn more than just what the worksheet is asking. You can learn that plus other things you start to think about and then you can choose to learn some more. It is a better way for everyone. We learned a lot." The audience is delighted to hear the wisdom of this young man. With an earnest story and example, he made our presenter's point by explaining the impact of digital learning and, more important, teacher-facilitated student choice.

Students were invited to present at this professional development session because the presenter asked whether any schools would be willing to bring students to the next session during his first of three meetings. Several schools from other districts volunteered to bring videos; however, we were fortunate to have a Transform Academy campus in attendance who could bring students. Our young man was followed by two other students with similar stories. They articulated how moving beyond the confines of worksheets, workbooks, and textbooks gave authenticity and purpose to learning. Learning was made relevant to their community, followed by the chance to demonstrate results of their work to peers and parents.

Although our students made live presentations, the videos from the other schools made similar and equally strong points. One campus interviewed middle school students about how they learned best, what types of activities made learning relevant, and what made going to class worthwhile. The themes were consistent:

- Collaborating with other students
- Accessing technology
- Having teachers who are good listeners
- Getting personalized lessons
- Being able to make mistakes and then correct them
- Having more choice regarding where they learn and how

With this information in hand, mind, and heart, our Transform Academy teachers began to realize that students were more than ready to accept innovative changes in the way school was conducted. They knew that the best of these innovations would require differentiated and innovative approaches to learning in the instructional environment along with giving students the opportunity to lead their own learning. Listening to students and encouraging their voices in a flexible learning environment would be the first step. Building relationships and teaching students how learning works would be key. Students needed a voice, choice, and flexibility in the classroom to move beyond accountability and standards and begin minding their own futures.

Promoting Differentiated Innovative Ideas

The third key component of the Emerging Vision is *differentiated innovative ideas* (see Figure 5.1). In this component, a **flexible learning environment** and **student-led learning** interrelate to strengthen achievement by giving students voice, choice, and leadership in the classroom. Our academy teachers were motivated by the research available to them in these areas, and they were excited to have the freedom to experiment with some of their ideas. To document and

Figure 5.1 Excerpt From Framework for Transforming a Learning Culture: Differentiated Innovative Ideas

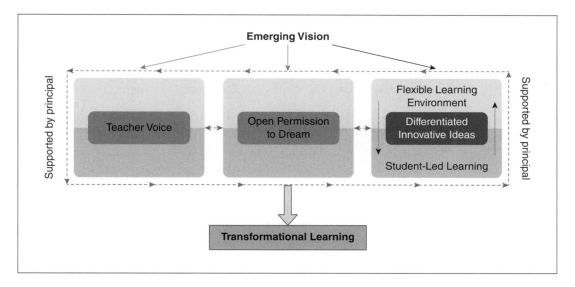

explore their enthusiastic endorsement of differentiated innovations, we have devoted Chapters 5 and 6 to this key component. We will examine the flexible learning environment in this chapter. Then this information will provide a launching pad for some deeper implementations regarding student-led learning in Chapter 6.

Encouraging Student Voice and Choice

Our teachers defined flexible learning environments as student-friendly places conducive to engaging learning experiences. To design spaces that were flexible and open to student growth, they needed to take time to hear what students wanted to say about both their physical and social learning environments, along with the learning choices they would like to make while in school. Thus, our teachers studied flexible learning environments from the aspects of student voice and choice. To gather essential information, they began conversations with students about how, when, and where learning takes place. Their queries included topics such as relationships with others, relevant learning needs, informative assessments, and inviting surroundings. During these conversations, the critical question our teachers asked their students was, "What makes learning interesting to you?"

Time to Collaborate!

Now is a good time to complete **Activity 5.1 What Does It Take to Engage Learners?** found at the end of this chapter.

As they gathered information from student conversations, it became apparent that not every student needed or preferred the same learning choices, tools, or paths. Innovative differentiation based on student voice and choice would provide learners the flexibility they needed to go beyond the standard curriculum and classroom walls. Let's examine our noteworthy flexible learning environment findings first from the perspective of student voice followed by student choice.

Student Voice

Their journey to find and intentionally listen to student voice led our teachers to understand that differentiating learning paths for individual students is one of the most challenging tasks many educators will encounter. To be a successful provider of engaging, personalized flexible learning, it is essential to gather information from not only other teachers and the research literature but from the students themselves. As teachers work to meet learning needs, their students provide ongoing data regarding the impact of instructional practices. Our teachers noted, for instance, their students gladly proposed some thought-provoking considerations about homework. This included preferred formats, types of feedback, grading standards, and their desire for group collaboration.

Our participants learned that an educator transitioning to a collaborative innovator mindset may begin lesson planning by giving students a preview of the next curriculum standards they will be undertaking, including the background knowledge needed for success. Next, our teacher would ask students for their ideas about some of the learning methods they would like to use to master the upcoming standards, as well as any challenges or concerns students may feel they will face. This information, in turn, would be shared during Professional Learning Community (PLC) meetings as part of the data to be used to plan student learning experiences.

To have meaningful conversations such as this with students, our Transform Academy teachers examined their relationships with their students and then asked questions about how students perceived their own learning process. This led the academy teachers to investigate methods for developing positive teacher-student relationships using open-ended discussions to learn about students' learning preferences. These conversations could be face-to-face, focus group style, or through surveys. In the true fashion of differentiation, various academy teachers found they had better results using either one or a combination of these approaches. The crucial idea was that they were listening!

Letting students know that their thoughts are important is essential for building positive teacher-student relationships. The Transform Academy recognized that when most teachers begin any new instructional approach, they start with experts, ask clarifying questions, and then incorporate this information into planning. Now the experts were students themselves! This is not always easy. Counting on student expertise can be difficult because teachers must recognize they are not the only experts in the room. By accepting that teachers are sometimes prone to making too many assumptions about student learning, the Transform Academy teachers decided to develop a way to systematically integrate student voice into learning decisions.

Our academy teachers knew that those who teach the same lesson, the same way year after year may not be differentiating for their learners or asking students how they learn best in today's world. Teachers who try new methods and remain open to suggestions will reach more students each time they cast a wider net of strategies. To assist the team and other teachers in gaining access to the personal learning preferences of students, our teachers worked collaboratively to develop steps for accessing student voice. The following suggestions are a summary of their findings:

- **Be intentional about learning from your students**.
  Plan your conversation format (face-to-face, survey, or focus group), make a clear set of questions, and keep a record what you have learned. Inform students why you are asking them questions and how you plan to use the information.

- **Understand, restate, and reflect**. Let students know that you hear them, restating what they say. Clearly inform them when you actually do use this information to improve their personal learning.

- **Decide where to begin to personalize learning**. Plan where in the curriculum you will begin to personalize learning. Design your plan around what the students need to know, the strategies they prefer for learning, and the way they will know when they have met their learning goals.

- **Give students clear expectations and boundaries.** When beginning your plan, be sure students understand the expectations for both personal learning and conduct in this type of learning environment.

- **Review plans and outcomes with students regularly.** At preset times, review student outcomes and modify plans and strategies as needed. Let students know you are open to listening to their suggestions and concerns during feedback opportunities.

- **Repeat the process as a continuous cycle.** Keep your students informed regarding strategies that are working and those you are considering, beginning with step one in this process. Keep the door open to new conversations by letting them know you are available to listen.

The teacher participants summed up their work on student voice with the following thoughts. First, students have much to contribute and they want to be heard. Everything can be personalized today and individualized learning is now expected and needed. Second, part of a teacher's job is to mindfully and intentionally observe, listen, and talk to students. Third, it is not necessary for a teacher to know how to reach all learners; however, learners should be given opportunities to provide additional information about themselves as they converse with the teacher. Actually, it really has never been a teacher's job to know all; somewhere along the way a teacher's job became the "all-knowing one" instead of a facilitator of learning. A successful learning experience begins with a collaborative teacher-student relationship.

Including student voice in learning is not a one-time event. It is a cycle with a multitude of outcomes and strategies that, when implemented, are meant to assist students in achieving success. A teacher's job is to persevere through the process of encouraging student voice so that students achieve optimal results through personalized learning. Listening to students and acting upon their ideas establishes a flexible learning culture that transforms a student's school experience. Listening may come in many forms, including conversations, surveys, and group conferences.

The academy participants appreciated that successful teachers understand there are definite observable differences in the ways students learn. Thus, a teacher cannot compel students to learn using only one teaching method. There are many times when students need to take the reins and decide for themselves how best to approach the tasks. Deciding how to incorporate students' learning preferences becomes a great opportunity for a PLC to discuss lesson designs using differentiated approaches. A teacher needs to ask herself, other teachers, and her students what is required in the learning environment so that concepts are more easily internalized.

Our academy participants added that along with an openness to change, transformational learning requires an in-depth look at both instructional and procedural routines. Some of these are routines that teachers have always used, such as how to ask for help or manage classroom materials. However, with new learning environments we need to add new routines, including ways to schedule a meeting with teachers and peers, time management with a team, online etiquette, device selection, and how to set group norms in a PBL team to resolve conflicts and encourage one another. As the learning environment changes, teachers should be ready to observe classroom procedures carefully and work alongside students to establish routines, expectations, and boundaries. When students know their teacher and she knows them, moving into innovation is less stressful because everyone understands that routines are in place to make learning successful for all. As we listen and learn, experiment, and reflect on innovative differentiation, students will begin to grow and thrive in this new learning culture. Teachers become facilitators for student voices and provide guidance for student choice.

Time to Collaborate!

Now is a good time to complete **Activity 5.2 How Does the Environment Affect Learning?** found at the end of this chapter.

Student Choice

Within a personalized flexible learning experience, there are a variety of opportunities for student choice. To begin making learning choices, students need to understand their personal preferences. For example, some students may prefer auditory learning and others may favor learning visually. Similarly, some may wish to use a laptop and others may gravitate to smaller devices. One student may prefer to work alone for certain tasks while a classmate next to him blossoms in a collaborative group. Knowing their own learning preferences assists students as they make decisions regarding how to tackle curriculum standards and expectations.

Additionally, students enjoy choosing the physical setting for learning. This includes selections as simple as an elementary student sitting on a yoga ball all the way to upper level students convening a group in a living room–style hallway alcove. As they examined the facets of student choice, our Transform Academy teachers noted that although choice involves how a student approaches a learning activity, it also results in a variety of student-driven products to demonstrate mastery. Figure 5.2 outlines some types of student choice that our teachers observed.

Figure 5.2 Examples of Student Choice

Types of Student Choice	Examples
Learning Preferences	Auditory, visual, kinesthetic, sequential, random, abstract, concrete, inductive, deductive, discovery
Environment	Physical: seating, lighting, sounds, visuals, in class, out of class, colors Virtual: blogs, websites, eBooks Social: groups, individual
Tools	Paper based, laptops, tablets, phones, calculators
Collaboration	Groups, face-to-face, virtual, one-to-one, expert dialogues
Demonstrations of Mastery	Projects, assessments, demonstrations
Time	Arrangement of daily activities, order of learning events, sequence of subject areas, timing for independent and group work
Goal Setting	Daily targets, weekly benchmarks, final goals, data notebooks, graphs, self-reports

Student Learning Communities and Personalized Learning

So, how can student voice and choice take place with a room full of energetic learners? After research and discussion, the academy teachers suggested beginning with systematically implementing regularly scheduled small group instruction. Establishing what they termed *student learning communities* (SLC), they envisioned these groups functioning similarly to their own PLCs. Reasoning that although many teachers routinely teach using large group instruction mixed with occasional small groups, our teachers found research indicating students need to talk to each other regularly as they cooperatively learn and comprehend (Hattie, 2012). Our teachers discovered that classrooms filled with the sounds of student voices seemed more engaged than silent ones or ones where the teacher did most of the speaking.

The SLC establishes a collaborative environment in which students assist each other in the learning process. In this setting, teachers incorporate more student voice and choice by transforming their classrooms into student-centered environments. The teachers concluded that if adults like to work in collaborative environments around a table or sitting on couches with laptops, then students would be more comfortable in that same type of environment. This means that the physical arrangement of desks, tables, chairs, walls and dividers, and color require flexibility and variety. After experimenting with their physical environments, participants were excited to observe that the more comfortable students feel the more they want to settle in and learn. They found that how a classroom should look and feel is more about what students want than what makes a teacher comfortable or creating cute bulletin boards. It is about the well-being of students!

Imagine being an elementary student walking into the classroom of an innovative school district. As you look around you see there are no assigned desks; in fact, most of the colorful furniture is on wheels so that it can be easily moved about the room. The choices for seating include stools, rugs, a sofa, yoga balls, and even milk crates. Then the unthinkable happens: The teacher hands you markers and says, "As you work, you may write on these tables, this wall, and over here on the windows." There is a variety of technology to use and you can take it home! You think elementary school is great until you find yourself in the intermediate school. Now you not only have moveable furniture but you can adjust the work heights, and the tables collapse so the classroom can be rearranged quickly as you help your classmates determine the best design for the activities you will be doing. You are offered digital devices to use at school and at home or you can bring your own electronic tools. Finally, high school arrives. "Top my other schools," you think, as you enter a library coffee shop with booths for study groups and lots of soft seating. In this amazing world there are places to collaborate with other students around every corner, and teachers encourage you to use these areas. Classes do not meet every day, so you use these areas to work on projects with your SLC. All you need to do is check in with your teacher electronically. You can see through the walls and the school is open for all kinds of learners, with classes to prepare you for careers and higher education. Oh, and one more thing: charging stations and Wi-Fi for all of your electronics (even your phone) are plentiful. You never have a problem with bandwidth or a low battery. What a lucky student you are!

Teachers who successfully work in PLCs themselves find it is easier to plan for SLCs. These teachers are willing to allow students the opportunity to choose how they will express their learning. Students may select from an assortment of tools, media, and processes to achieve and then showcase their understanding of learning standards. Our teachers were careful to note that planning and student input are needed to accept and evaluate these varied approaches and outcomes. Regularly scheduled student conferences to check for progress and setting predetermined grading requirements are key. As learners are given a choice in how they will attain knowledge and how they will provide artifacts that demonstrate their new levels of understanding, it is important to remember that voice and choice still come with expectations.

When asked how they would demonstrate learning outcomes, our academy participants found students stepped up the challenge of choice. They produced artifacts that included videos, websites, blogs, digital portfolios, online games they designed and coded, and apps for cell phones and tablets. For example, elementary students showed they were capable of producing unexpected artifacts, such as videos with QR codes to show other students how to study for math tests. Intermediate students applied their knowledge of nutrition and good health by making presentations to elementary students online and in person. High school students worked in PBL groups to solve complex problems, such as ways to reduce noise pollution around airports while managing costs and ecological impact. Their presentations were professional enough to be placed online and provided in person to interested community groups.

Classrooms Growing Toward Flexible Learning Environments

When a teacher facilitates a flexible learning environment focusing on student voice and choice, then student engagement flourishes. The goal for the teachers in the Transform Academy was to become facilitators of personalized learning where student-centered activities are the norm, not the exception. Figure 5.3 presents the Characteristics of Classrooms Growing Toward Flexible Learning. Here learning situations may move across a continuum that proceeds from isolated student learning to SLCs on the horizontal axis. At the same time, a teacher's work moves on a continuum from status quo teacher-directed learning to innovative teacher-facilitated learning on the vertical axis. By intersecting the two continuums, a quadrant is formed similar to the one found in Chapter 2, Figure 2.1 Voices of Teachers Growing Toward Collaborative Innovation. In a differentiated innovative learning environment, the teacher's role becomes facilitative rather than directive. Student voice and choice take the lead as the teacher guides, advises, and remains open to various strategies for a variety of learners.

When learning occurs in isolation with a teacher who is focused on directing standardized lessons, most students have little chance of

Figure 5.3 Characteristics of Classrooms Growing Toward Flexible Learning

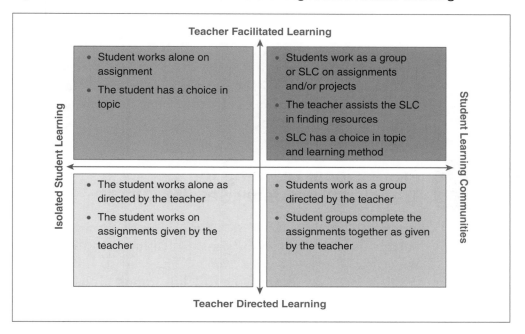

deeply internalizing their learning. Teachers who direct learning in a standardized method but allow for frequent collaboration among the students are taking steps towards facilitating deep learning by allowing student voice in the teacher-directed SLC. The teacher who offers student choice but does not allow for collaborative learning is also moving positively toward personalized learning but missing the mark by not increasing student-to-student communication.

As our academy teachers remade their physical classrooms and rebooted their instructional methods, they were reminded that teachers in a personalized learning environment witness learners in adjustment phases, just as they were doing in the Transform Academy. Some students, just like some teachers, do not like to collaborate. Sometimes this is because a student fears that others will find out that he or she has trouble learning, and it is challenging to admit that learning is difficult. Teachers who develop relationships with students and use personal learning methods are keenly aware of this. They encourage students by modeling positive interactions so that when they are ready, students enter an SLC with confidence. The academy teachers knew that new learning rarely takes place when someone is alone all the time either physically, socially, or virtually. Some learning may come from individual study, but most learning is language connected and thus comprehended best through relevant collaborative activities.

After adding student voice and choice to their own classrooms, our academy teachers articulated their findings: "When students have a relationship with their teacher and the opportunity to make learning choices then they become invested in their learning. This results in students who internalize and retain what they have worked so hard to learn and comprehend." For example, teachers found that across a semester they did fewer reviews of prior learning and students recalled background knowledge with less assistance.

Professional Learning for Transform Academy Session 7

Our research and field trips to study flexible learning environments brought us back to two of our early and defining questions. First, *What does it take to engage learners?* and second, *How does the environment affect learning?* During this session of the academy, we sought to learn from our academy participants their thoughts about the learning environment and the innovative steps they were taking to engage students through flexible surroundings and collaborative arrangements.

Comfort, Color, Choice, and Collaboration

As the teachers conducted research related to their professional learning plans, they discovered a new area of interest that needed further study: the physical learning environment. As learners, they could relate to what they had read; a comfortable chair to sit in during a professional development session was certainly a plus! After thinking about their own learning, they began to wonder if the same applied to students in the classroom.

Questions from academy teachers did not stop with the kinds of chairs that were available for student use in the classroom. They began wondering whether different types of desks might impact the levels of student engagement and learning. Reflecting on their field trip to the Career and Technical Education classrooms, they could certainly see how the physical environment of the classroom allowed for the type of collaborative interactions necessary for authentic engagement and success. The field trip to the architect firm not only confirmed the importance of the types of furniture available for students but also made them think about the use of color in the classroom. Once again, the facilitators of the academy were eager to listen to the voices of these

Figure 5.4 How to Repurpose Materials Easily at Hand

Discarded Item	Repurposed
Tables	• all shapes and heights that could be adjusted into low tables • allow for colorful pillows on the floor for seating
Desks	• with some adjustments could be raised so that a student could stand while focusing on tasks • by removing the legs could become a lap desk allowing a student to sit on the floor, cushion, or pillow
Bookcases	• could serve multiple, creative purposes such as dividers with the plain side painted with chalkboard paint • a perfect tool for collaborative teamwork projects
Shelves	• with a coat of paint so the teachers could use color to designate types of work areas or storage for supplies
Two-drawer file cabinets	• could be used to create an L-shaped work area separated from other areas in the room • flat vertical surface could be painted with dry erase paint to create another area for small groups to create and display their thinking
Trapezoid-shaped tables	• refinish the surface with dry erase paint after sanding and smoothing out the rough/notched surface

innovative teachers and respond accordingly. Based on the teachers' enthusiasm and ideas for new classroom designs, the academy facilitators arranged for a tour of the district warehouse and helped smooth the bureaucratic process of using repurposed materials already owned by the district, including ensuring that the "new" furniture met all safety guidelines. In this way, the academy facilitators, employees of the school district, served as aides to implement teachers' innovative ideas rather than as roadblocks. Figure 5.4 lists examples of what teachers discovered during their tour of the warehouse.

NOTE: *It was important that the maintenance department and the safety officer for the district were involved in the transformations taking place in the classrooms. There were lots of lessons to be learned regarding the use of the chalkboard and dry erase paint on various surfaces in the classroom, including the walls. They were excited to see a repurposing of furniture and worked diligently with the teachers to ensure a safe learning environment for students.*

Although these changes may seem simple, there were shifts in the ways the classroom space was arranged and utilized. The thoughtful planning for an environment that encouraged communication and collaboration was evident as student voice and choice made way for collaboration, PBL, and unique ways to demonstrate learning outcomes. Walkthroughs in these classrooms positively reflected the results teachers had intended.

The trip to the warehouse was just the beginning of the changes the teachers wanted in their classrooms. As you might imagine, the changes required funds. Teachers became very creative problem solvers! They submitted proposals to the district's education foundation. Requests were also submitted to the parent organizations in the schools as well as online donor sites. This cohort of teachers was committed to making changes in the types of furniture for their classrooms and were willing to complete the required paperwork in order to achieve the desired changes.

The field trips to the architect firm and a technology conference brought the teachers in close contact with vendors—and they took full advantage of the opportunity! Some of the participants contacted the vendors directly and were able to get samples sent to their campuses. They had a chance to actually observe their students using the furniture and could make decisions based on their observations. This provided an excellent opportunity to try out the product. Again, in response to teachers' voices, the academy put on a Vendor Fair, which gave the academy teachers a close look at the types of furniture they wanted to see in their classrooms.

Catalogues were shared during one of the academy sessions and the teachers browsed through, marking the items they wanted to examine at the Vendor Fair. The event was scheduled over a two-day period and the teachers were encouraged to attend with their principals. Some of the teachers spoke with parents of students and asked them to attend as well. This would give them the chance to listen to their students' comments about the items as well as determine the comfort level of the items. While they were viewing the furniture and other items from the catalogs, they could visit with the representatives from the company to discuss color, size, and any other options that were available. A survey was developed that each teacher completed while visiting each vendor's booth. This information became a valuable tool as the district planned for purchases at new campuses and revitalization at other campuses.

The Vendor Fair had a great impact on the teachers and students as they planned for learning environments. During a professional learning session, there was an opportunity to hear first-hand from 10 students ranging from elementary through high school about their preferences in learning. Even a recent graduate joined the panel. She expressed her unbiased perspective and reflections about her learning experiences in the past as well as her college experience.

The students shared what they believed would make learning more engaging for them in the classroom. As expected, they included many of the topics the teachers were researching such as comfort, color, choice, and collaboration. They wanted more project-based experiences instead of what they referred to as drill and kill. Since they were good students, they expressed how compliance was their usual mode of operation and, because they truly liked and respected their teachers, they followed along with the teachers' requests. The panel experience gave them the permission to express their opinions about optimal ways of personalized learning.

Throughout the years the students heard the phrase "college and career ready." During the panel discussion, they expressed that they did not feel that sitting in rows and working in isolation was preparing them to become college or career ready. They knew that in the real world they were going to have to work in teams with other people to solve challenges in their college courses and new jobs. They wanted to talk with their peers and discuss important issues—things that were relevant to them. If engaged learners was the intended outcome, then students expressed that they needed choice in their learning opportunities.

With each monthly session it seemed as though the academy teachers were more intent on making shifts in the teaching and learning that was taking place in their classrooms. The sessions allowed them to learn about and experience some of the innovative practices they wanted to pursue in their own classrooms. As one might imagine, they could become overwhelmed by all the possibilities. Through the use of Activities 5.1 and 5.2, their personal learning plans (PLPs) were revisited. This not only would insure a continued focus on implementing the actions stated in their plans but would allow for changes in the plans as a result of the ongoing learning that was taking place. The academy teachers were encouraged to make the adjustments. It was critical that each plan would remain a reflection of their individual voices.

KEY IDEAS

At this point in the Transform Academy timeline, the teachers have discovered a vital component in transformative learning: listening to the student. Simultaneously, through implementation of research-based ideas, teachers found that student voice and choice leads to the establishment of student learning communities (SLC). The SLC, as well as color and comfort in the learning environment, are the ultimate results of the collaborative partnership between the teacher and students.

DISCUSSION QUESTIONS

1. How is student voice used to guide decision making in the learning culture?

2. How is student choice supported in the PLC planning process?

3. How will teachers and principals collaborate in order to make changes in comfort, color, choice, and collaboration in their environments?

Transform Academy Session 7 Activities

ACTIVITY 5.1 WHAT DOES IT TAKE TO ENGAGE LEARNERS?

Intended Outcome: To provide an opportunity for participants to discuss their beliefs related to the causes of student disengagement and to connect their ideas with their personal learning plans

Preparation: Arrange the training area so that there are four large areas available for participants to sit comfortably while completing the group activities. Sticky notes and pencils should be available for each group at the tables. Chart paper or large sheets of paper should be available for each group.

Please visit http://resources.corwin.com/MindingTheFuture to access the online resources for this book.

Facilitation:

1. The facilitator opens the discussion by asking participants to think about the following question: What are the main causes of students' lack of engagement in the classroom?

   a. Provide ample time for participants to reflect and respond to the question individually. Each response should be written on a sticky note. In silence, each group should post the sticky notes on the chart paper designated for the group.

   b. As the participants read the responses on each sticky note, they should look for ideas that are connected and place the ideas in categories. Ideas can be moved from one category to another by any member of the group. The sticky notes may be moved numerous times until group members are satisfied with the results.

   c. To complete the task, each group should label each category on the chart.

   d. Using the Online Resource T.1 graphic organizer, participants insert the label for each cluster of ideas in the cloud shape on the document.

2. As the small groups share with the larger group, the participants should look and listen for similarities in their responses and the categories.

3. Working in the same groups, the participants select one of the labels assigned to a cluster of ideas and begin searching for related ideas in the visioning document. As they find articles or premises of the visioning document that align to each concept, the participants should record the information next to the bullets under each cloud.

4. Once the alignment between each concept and the visioning document has been determined, the individual participants should begin reviewing their personal learning plans using Online Resource T.2. As they review the plans they need to reflect on the following:

   • Is there an alignment between the concept and your personal learning plan? If so, what progress has been made so far?

   • If there is not an alignment, should this concept be included in your personal learning plan? What evidence will you need in order to determine the level of progress?

5. Once the participants have completed the review process, each campus team should meet to discuss the current status of their personal learning plans as well as plans for continued progress.

Parts of Activity 5.1 have been adapted from *Thinking Through Quality Questioning* (Walsh & Sattes, 2011).

ACTIVITY 5.2 HOW DOES THE ENVIRONMENT AFFECT LEARNING?

Intended Outcome: To provide an opportunity for participants to learn more about comfort, color, choice, and collaboration and how each affects learning in the classroom

Preparation: Print handout of statements for each participant from Online Resource U.1, prepare statement posters from Online Resource U.2 and post around the room. Sticky notes should be available for participants. Select four articles for the jigsaw activity and make copies available for the group (one article focused on color in the classroom or school, one article focused on comfort in the classroom, one article focused on choice in the classroom, and a final article focused on collaboration in the classroom)

Figure 5.5 Bar Graph Example

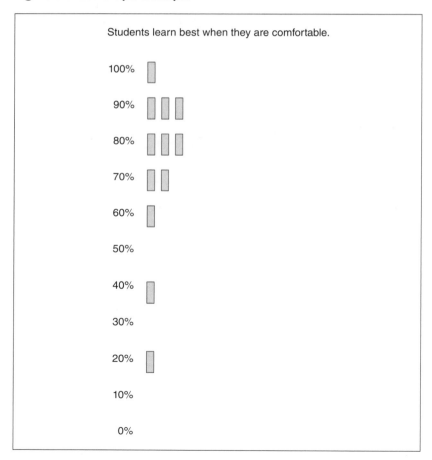

Facilitation:

1. The participants should read each question on the Online Resource U.1 handout of statements and indicate the extent to which they agree (from 0% to 100%).

2. Once completed, the participants should indicate their responses on the statement posters by placing sticky notes next to the appropriate response. A bar graph will be formed as the responses are placed on the chart (see Figure 5.5).

3. As the participants view the charts they should begin forming conclusions. Provide additional time for the participants to ask questions of one another as well as discuss their conclusions.

4. Distribute the articles to the participants at each table. Be sure that all four articles are being read by at least one person at each table.

5. Ask participants to reorganize so that they meet in expert groups (i.e., with other participants who have the same article). Each group should read the article, discuss the important concepts, and determine the key points/ideas to share when they return to their home groups.

6. After sufficient time, participants return to their original home groups in order to teach one another what they have learned.

7. Facilitate a whole-class discussion to form connections between the articles and the posters as well as the implications of the new learning.

Parts of Activity 5.2 have been adapted from *Thinking Through Quality Questioning* (Walsh & Sattes, 2011).

Suggested Action Items

Action Items	Progress Checks			
1. Review steps taken from the last chapter. Make planning adjustments and communication updates as needed.	☐ Not started	☐ In progress	☐ Completed	☐ NA
2. Form a team to consider learning environment changes:				
• Long-range plans of campus and district	☐ Not started	☐ In progress	☐ Completed	☐ NA
• Budgets and possible funding sources	☐ Not started	☐ In progress	☐ Completed	☐ NA
• Safety and ADA guidelines	☐ Not started	☐ In progress	☐ Completed	☐ NA
• Strategic plans	☐ Not started	☐ In progress	☐ Completed	☐ NA
3. Prioritize your needs and complete the professional learning activities in this chapter.				
• Activity 5.1 What Does It Take to Engage Learners?	☐ Not started	☐ In progress	☐ Completed	☐ NA
• Activity 5.2 How Does the Environment Affect Learning?	☐ Not started	☐ In progress	☐ Completed	☐ NA
4. Continue to schedule time to assist teachers with personal learning plans.	☐ Not started	☐ In progress	☐ Completed	☐ NA
5. Review calendars for study, meeting, journaling, data checks, and communicating results.	☐ Not started	☐ In progress	☐ Completed	☐ NA

CHAPTER 6

Student-Led Learning

Session 8

I have no special talents. I am only passionately curious.

—**ALBERT EINSTEIN (1952)**

Getting Acquainted With This Chapter

Student leadership in the classroom, extracurricular activities, and community-based organizations are invaluable educational opportunities. In addition, expanded leadership expertise will be required from students in their future occupations. Teachers sometimes resist student leadership in the learning process because of the established norm of the teacher as the provider of information. Transform Academy teachers courageously adapt as they become facilitators of learning instead of providers of knowledge. In this chapter, we illustrate what happens to the learning culture when student-led learning is prioritized and affirmed.

Teachers Learn to Code

Imagine a third-grade girl wearing a floral summer dress and rhinestone-studded sandals as she confidently steps forward to help a struggling teacher. She reaches across a table and quickly taps on the teacher's computer keyboard and says, "There it is. See, nothing is lost. You just need to keep trying to finish this side of the program. You can get it when you loop back into what you already know. It is just like when you help me with math problems!" Meanwhile, one of her team members approaches another teacher. He pats her on the shoulder and asks whether she needs any help. The teacher replies, "I am having fun learning but I just need more time with this part of the code. Learning new things takes time!"

Across the school cafeteria, upper grade elementary students are conducting a morning of professional learning for the 40 faculty members at their school. A line of parents across the back of the room sitting in green and orange plastic chairs smile as they watch their children dressed in their Sunday best teach their teachers how to write computer code. The faculty started their day knowing they would be attending training with guest presenters who would be giving them some great new ideas. They were surprised to see the school's Coding Club waiting for them with serious, bright faces ready to embark upon an important and timely mission: involving everyone in the school in learning to write computer code using a coding challenge such as the Hour of Code sponsored by Code.org. The principal and club sponsor were their allies in this mission. Weeks earlier, they guided the passionate group of young coders in the creation of a step-by-step plan to teach everyone in the school to code. First, train the faculty; next, introduce coding to the student body Grades K–5; and then follow up with encouragement and prizes for tutorial hours accomplished. They set lofty goals with high expectations of success.

It is no surprise this group of code-loving students, their supportive principal, and Transform Academy teacher sponsor quickly gain the endorsement of the faculty. The students begin their teacher training by demonstrating their coding projects built during the campus's afterschool coding club. After detailing what coding means to them, the students give their teachers a tour of the coding website and show an introductory video that begins with a Steve Jobs quote, "Everyone in the country should learn to program a computer because it teaches you how to think."

Using digital slides, the students explain what this quote means to them. A colorful graphic flashes the words, "Metacognition and Iterative Thinking." Then the students give their own definition of these words, "We must be ready to learn new things and this means that we need to know how to think and use new ways to solve problems. When one idea doesn't work then we need to go back and look for mistakes and ways to fix our work." The faculty indulgently smiles at their wonderful students and open their laptops to begin their hour of code. By the end of the morning, 40 teachers have completed one hour of coding. The first goal is accomplished!

During the following days and weeks, students across the campus take the one hour of code challenge with the encouragement of their teachers and the coding club members. The next events astonish the faculty. Students commandeer their parents' home computers and start learning on their own. The goal-breaking hours of coding accumulate, and from these inspired students we learn that when learning is relevant and personalized, students will engage!

Websites such as Code.org demonstrate how a personalized learning path, choice, and goal setting can be used to fully engage learners. Within the coding tutorials, students choose from a variety of engaging environments, such as the latest movie themes, or enter "play labs" designed to teach coding fundamentals in a colorful, nonjudgmental environment. Following the tutorials, students may select from a list of full coding courses for more advanced learning in areas that include programming languages and building apps, games, and websites.

Coding Clubs were a wonderful yet unintended consequence of the Transform Academy. Opening the door to innovative ideas encourages emerging visions of what school can really be when everyone collaborates, communicates, learns, and leads.

Fostering Student-Led Learning

In Chapter 5, we began the exploration of differentiated innovative ideas by focusing on how a flexible learning environment gives students voice and choice (see Figure 5.1). We examined our Transform Academy teachers' recommendations for intentionally accessing student voice by using student-teacher conferencing and surveys to gather information about learning preferences and engagement in school. We also discovered the ways these conversations influenced our academy teachers to use comfort, color, and choice when designing collaborative learning environments. Beyond their physical environments, our academy teachers studied how moving to student learning communities (SLCs) and teacher-facilitated learning creates an environment where differentiated innovative ideas flourish (see Figure 5.3, Characteristics of Classrooms Growing Toward Flexible Learning). In this chapter, we will present how our teachers implemented student-led learning using differentiated innovative ideas.

Figure 6.1 Excerpt From Framework for Transforming a Learning Culture: Differentiated Innovative Ideas

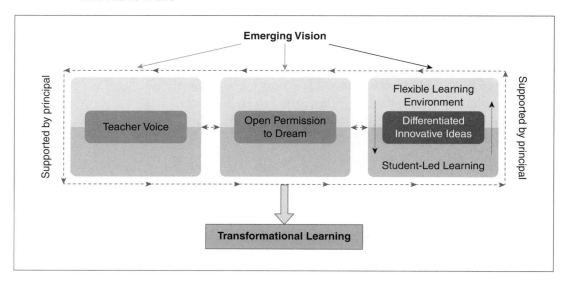

Essentials for Implementing Student-Led Learning

Moving an emerging vision forward means implementing differentiated innovative ideas that prioritize student leadership. As our teachers grew from being content directors to learning facilitators, they discerned that in addition to teaching a standards-based curriculum they also needed to understand the social and emotional needs of learners. Through this study, they discovered strategies to assist students with the self-knowledge required to lead, influence, and improve their own learning. As our academy teachers narrowed their findings, four aspects essential to developing student-led learning surfaced: student influence, affirmation of students, cooperative environments, and deliberate refinement.

Time to Collaborate!

Now is a good time to complete **Activity 6.1 Honing Our Craft**, found at the end of this chapter.

Student Influence

During their innovative classroom work, our teachers recognized the necessity of student influence in learning outcomes. Although they knew that students were increasingly aware of how they learn best, there were still times learners needed guidance to articulate their needs. To shift the instructional focus from one size fits all to individual learners, our teachers began to structure opportunities for intentional and frequent conversations with students. During these conversations, teachers assisted learners in finding the best ways to successfully demonstrate mastery of curriculum content.

Before we continue, let's look at an example of a conversation between a teacher and a group her students where students feel comfortable asking about options for an upcoming assignment.

Student A: What format will you accept for the law project?

Student B: Yeah, does it need to be typed, double-spaced, in Times New Roman and 12-point font?

Teacher: Well, what are you thinking?

Student C: I would like to make a chart that compares the advantages and disadvantages of the law.

Teacher: That will work.

Student C: Yes! (She smiles and gives a thumbs up sign.)

Student D: What if we want to look at the law from another person's viewpoint?

Teacher: Describe it to me and we can chat online.

Teacher: (Looking at the whole group). Have you ever thought about using an electronic mind map to show your thinking? You could color code your thoughts.

Student A: We can really do that instead of a paper?

Teacher: Of course, if it makes sense to you and you have covered your rubric metrics.

Student B: Would you please ask our other teachers to have this kind of discussion about product choice?

Teacher: (Smiling to herself) I sure will at our next PLC when I show the team what you can really do. And for those of you who seem to be inspired at the last minute, remember a midnight CST electronic timestamp counts.

Our teachers began their conversations with one small group at a time. They got to know their students then moved to the next group. This took some time, but they soon established routines to reach all learners on a regular basis and to be available when students needed to meet, whether in person or online. You may think electronic communication was only available for upper grade students; however, elementary students happily chatted electronically with their teachers about assignments and homework.

The presence of a teacher facilitator during SLCs aids in accelerating student influence in the learning environment. As small groups of students collaborate to lead their own learning, the teacher is present to assist with optimal learning by systematically checking learning progress and group dynamics. In their SLCs, students moved beyond the established curriculum and explored new ways of approaching concepts, such as examining how weather impacts the economy. Technology helped students step out of their textbooks and work as a team to evaluate online information, investigate current research, and then collaboratively develop a model demonstrating the positive and negative influences of weather on their own city. When students in an SLC take responsibility to accomplish team goals, former competitors became cooperative allies!

As they discussed the impact of SLCs on student learning, our academy teachers reasoned with their PLC peers, "If teachers collaborate to improve their professional learning, why would we not allow students the same process?" To maximize student influence in innovative learning, our teachers believed that they must facilitate conversations with their students, support student-led learning, and become enthusiastic supporters of transformation in their own PLCs.

Affirmation of Students

As students gradually assume responsibility for their own learning, whether in independent work or in an SLC, teacher and peer affirmation are supportive keys for growth. Our teachers employed their instructional facilitator skills to affirm student learning preferences and provide guidance to set and accomplish goals.

Using methods such as conversations, surveys, and face-to-face meetings, teachers acknowledge student learning styles and preferences. This knowledge is further championed when teachers and SLC members become a support team for one another. For example, when a student is not ready to work in an SLC and voices a preference to work in isolation while listening to music, our academy teachers determined they could take gradual steps to guide such students to work in an SLC. To begin, they recognized and honored this preference when possible. This may include some time for mastery of skills, such as learning the steps to divide fractions or science safety rules. Next, students were encouraged to work on a short-term small group assignment with one or two other students who also liked to listen to music. This group may spend 30 minutes collaboratively solving a set of math problems. By meeting both curriculum and social goals, students begin to see the supportive value of an SLC. The role of the teacher is to observe and affirm these changes.

Goal setting creates personal connections to new content and skills. This translates into engagement and pride in learning outcomes. Our academy participants outlined the essential steps for goal setting in this way. Upon discussing upcoming learning standards with students, individual or team conferences are scheduled. In preparation for these conferences, students define what they understand they will be learning, what they already know about the topic, the outcomes or products needed to demonstrate new knowledge, and the steps they will take to accomplish their goals. During the meeting, teachers review these elements with students and assist with goal setting. Through this process, students gain clarity about the purpose of their work and how goals will be accomplished before a project begins. Looking back to our story at the beginning of this chapter, we see this in action. Students took ownership of their learning, designed a method to demonstrate this learning, and set an admirable goal to complete their project: everyone will code for an hour. On their team-developed rubric they rated their own progress during the project. Across the timeline of their project, they moved from beginning coders (starting to learn) to intermediate (needs help sometimes) then expert (works alone) and finally to their pinnacle: coding teacher!

Cooperative Environment

When you change the arrangement of furniture in your living room, it may take some time to acclimate, but as research shows, change is ultimately good for the brain. You sit in a different place and suddenly say to yourself, "Why didn't I do this sooner?" Similarly, our academy teachers found that as furniture moves around in a classroom, academic and social-emotional growth increases. In a cooperative learning environment, trusting others and valuing their innovative ideas develops shared responsibility and mutual respect.

Some innovations involve risk. In these cases, trust is essential because risk opens us to being vulnerable (Combs, Edmonson, Harris, 2013). In the experiences of our participants, trust developed between students, teachers, and principals through regular collaboration, trying new ideas, celebrating the successes, and making improvements. Being there for each other while honoring feedback is necessary to build trust as the status quo is rearranged. Fear of failure when creating a cooperative learning environment is very real, and both students and their teacher have much on the line as they build confidence in one another to implement new ideas.

For a teacher moving toward collaborative innovation, taking a risk to give students classroom leadership is not easy. Further, imagine students who have always been told exactly how and when to complete an assignment being asked to make decisions about how they can best learn new material. Sometimes we all want someone to just tell us what to do and let us move on with our day. But as someone once said, "Nothing ventured, nothing gained." What better way to develop new ideas than to value and trust students to try something different that they believe will help them achieve their learning goals?

A cooperative environment encourages everyone to participate in transforming learning. Our teachers involved the students in redesigning the look and functionality of their classrooms. They asked students about lighting, furniture heights, and schedules. Then participants turned to product designs and assessments. During goal-setting conferences, they gave students choice boards for projects and included students' opinions in evaluation rubrics. Changes like this took time, with several cycles of critical thinking and idea exchanges, to reach a point where trust developed and creative thinking was valued. When this environment is maintained, teacher facilitators support student-led learning, create trusting relationships, and value new ideas.

Deliberate Refinement

Experimentation with new ideas such as goal-setting conferences permits students to cooperatively share responsibility for leading changes. Therefore, if some new ideas are not optimally implemented, the next step is for a teacher to facilitate a decision-making process for deliberate refinement, during which students review results and brainstorm possibilities. It is possible for a group using this process to find that there are ideas that benefit some individuals while others need something else. For example, when our teachers began using student conferencing to set learning goals, some students expressed that they were more comfortable meeting online while others loved the one-to-one time with their teacher. To build trust in these conferences, our teachers used students' preferred communication method first and then gradually challenged students to use other meeting techniques.

During transformation there are many moments of success, while at other times we realize improvement is needed. In fact, teachers found that most of their successful ideas usually needed some tweaking. Further, they realized that developing a regular process, such as PLC and SLC meetings, was essential to the deliberate refinement of new ideas. The principal assisted with establishing an expectation for regular PLC meetings, and teachers followed a similar model in their classroom SLCs. Note taking during professional and student meetings helped teams to repeat successes and reflect on improvements. Deliberate reflection needs to be a regularly scheduled and supported event for teachers and principals.

As with the completion of a puzzle, all the pieces of student influence, affirmation of students, cooperative environments, and deliberate refinement began to fit together. The order and ways in which they occurred varied by the individual learners and teacher facilitators involved. The most important aspect was to begin! It was not perfect at first, but when students took responsibility for their learning and were a collaborative part of the classroom processes, excitement replaced the need for classroom standardization. When differentiated innovative ideas are implemented, along with teacher voice and open permission to dream, a vision emerges and transformative learning happens. Our Transform Academy members took this leap and were rewarded with students who were more deeply engaged in learning.

Professional Learning for Transform Academy Session 8

During this session, we continued our work with differentiated innovative ideas by exploring student-led learning. Learning from the students requires asking the right questions in a risk-free environment. We explored the use of surveys, face-to-face meetings, and shadowing students in different learning environments to gather learner feedback regarding learning preferences and levels of engagement.

Learning From Students

Because working as a PLC was the norm for the Transform Academy teachers, we began the session with a quick review of the four essential questions they were in the practice of asking and responding to:

1. What is it we want our students to learn?
2. How will we know whether each student has learned it?
3. How will we respond when some students do not learn it?
4. How can we extend and enrich the learning for students who have demonstrated proficiency? (DuFour, DuFour, Eaker, & Many, 2006)

This brief discussion provided a segue for asking the participants to ponder the next question: How are the four essential questions and practices to support student engagement in learning different and how are they similar? (See Online Resource Y.1 and Activity 6.1.)

As the participants worked in their small groups, they realized they had not made the intentional connection between student engagement and their responses to the four questions in their work as campus PLCs. This resulted in a lively discussion and valuable written responses. After sharing their responses with the whole group, the teachers were asked to consider the following questions:

1. Looking at both areas of focus, who is typically in control of the information and actions in that area? Why is that so?

2. How might you go about learning the students' thoughts and ideas related to student engagement?

3. How does/might your personal learning plan address these issues?

The discussion was thought provoking and, as you can imagine, often led to more questions that needed to be answered. Based on their experiences thus far, teachers knew that feedback from students could be a powerful tool, but they weren't certain *how* to get that feedback from students. Once they shared their findings with the whole group, it was apparent the idea of incorporating student voice into their practices would require some thoughtful planning and action.

As they looked for ways to engage learners, the teachers realized this not only would allow them to hone in on their practices but would also take their personal learning plans to a deeper level of implementation. No longer were they going to use the research conducted by others as their only source of information. If they wanted to learn what engages their students they needed to *ask their students*.

Using Surveys

The starting point for some of the teachers was to conduct surveys to determine students' perceptions regarding instruction and teacher practices in their own classrooms. Working in small groups during the session, the academy teachers discussed the elements they wanted to address in the survey.

With Figure 6.2 as a foundation for their questions, they completed searches for examples of student surveys. Using several different sample

Figure 6.2 **Four Areas Essential to Integrating Student Voice**

Student Influence	Affirmation of Students
• Conversations between teacher and student	• Support of student learning preferences and setting learning goals
• Collaboration between students	• Encouragement of student independence
Cooperative Environment	**Deliberate Refinement**
• Experimentation with new ideas	• Exchange of success and improvement
• Value and trust	• Regular reflection

surveys, they crafted questions that would provide valuable information to assist them in adjusting their practices. Online Resource V provides links to various student survey resources.

In their usual manner, they wanted to return to their classrooms the next day and provide the survey to their students. They also wanted the support of their academy colleagues as they planned the adjustments they would make in their classrooms. Because they would not be together as a group for another month, they decided to share their results using an electronic file storage system (e.g., Google Drive, Dropbox). This would enable them to view the results, collaborate with one another, and identify possible next steps, including sharing the results with their students.

Face-to-Face Meetings

While some of the teachers planned to begin their investigation using student surveys, others wanted to focus their initial efforts on face-to-face meetings with students. Whether this was in a 1:1 setting or in a student panel format at lunch or recess, the teachers began their investigation by determining what they hoped to learn from their students. This seemed to be the logical starting point for them because this is how they often began their work in PLCs on campus. Figure 6.2 Four Areas Essential to Integrating Student Voice was once again used to narrow the focus of the questions they would use in their conversations with the students. Much like the previous group, they browsed through the available professional texts and conducted Internet searches. They discovered they could utilize questions found in many student surveys, with some adjustments. They developed questions aligned to each area on the chart, allowing each teacher to select the questions that aligned to the current needs. Online Resource W provides questions to use in the face-to-face meeting.

Once the questions were developed, they needed to create a plan for implementing the interviews at their individual campuses. In campus teams, they responded to the following questions:

- How will we update our principal on this plan?
- How many students should we interview?
- How will we select the students?
- How many students should be included in the student panels?
- When will we meet with the students?
- What is our deadline for completing the interviews?
- When will we meet to discuss our findings?
- How will we follow up with students after the interviews?

It was important for the campus team to create a schedule and a timeline for conducting the interviews because each teacher was responsible for conducting the interviews with the students of one of his or her academy colleagues. Each teacher also selected the questions pertinent to her classroom to include in the interviews. Although this required a coordinated effort, they felt confident the results of the interviews would lead to meaningful changes in the ways they would engage students in learning.

Shadowing Students for a Day

The last group of colleagues decided to begin their investigation by shadowing students, a process that involves following a student or students through all or part of the school day in order to gain insight regarding the learning experiences in each classroom. This process would enable them to better understand their own instructional practices and ways they engage students in the learning process.

They began their discussion focused on what they wanted to discover about their students' learning experiences in their colleagues' classrooms. They determined that although student engagement could look different in various content areas, there were some similarities across all areas. Figure 6.2 Four Areas Essential to Integrating Student Voice could be used once again as a springboard for developing an observational tool for shadowing the students. A sample of the observational tool for shadowing a student is located in Online Resource X.

Once the observational tool was created they broke into campus teams. Each teacher selected two to three students to shadow. Although the majority of the teachers selected students who would be representative of students in the class as a whole, several teachers selected students they were most concerned about, in hopes of gaining more insight into their overall performance in other classrooms. After reviewing each student's schedule, they worked as a campus team to create a schedule that would allow all of the selected students in one teacher's classroom to be observed by one of the academy teachers. They attempted to position the shadowing teacher in classrooms where she could observe two or three of the students simultaneously. As you can imagine, developing the schedule was a time-consuming task but well worth the effort.

Although they were well on their way to a successful shadowing experience, there were still a few issues that needed to be resolved. Before moving forward with their plan, they needed to

- Share the plan with the principal and seek input for improvements

- Confirm the acquisition of substitutes with the principal

- Share the purpose of shadowing with the classroom teachers of the shadowed students

- Determine how each observer would conduct a conversation with each of the shadowed students after the observations were completed

- Schedule a time to meet and discuss the observations as well as information gleaned in the student conversations after the observation

- Develop a plan for sharing their findings with the principal

Once the shadowing experience was completed, they would take time to reflect on their learning from the experience. Using their reflections, they would develop a plan for implementing changes in their classrooms and act on the plan.

Just as we had seen so many times throughout the year, the academy teachers were willing to provide optimal learning environments for their students. They believed the students had something to teach each of us and, uncomfortable as it may be, they were prepared to listen to the students' voices regardless of what students said and act on the findings with grace and fidelity. The use of surveys, face-to-face meetings, and shadowing students would provide valuable feedback to inform instructional practices that lead to student engagement.

Teachers were placed in a unique position during the innovative process to choose the role of facilitator as they prioritized student leadership in learning. Students expressed their need for choice; personalization; and a comfortable, colorful environment for learning (just to mention a few). As a result, teachers saw students who were highly engaged in their learning. This was just the tip of iceberg during Session 8 when the Transform Academy teachers opened the door to student-led learning.

DiSCUSSiON QUESTiONS

1. What opportunities do you provide for students to lead learning?

2. What is the process for students to have choice in the learning process?

3. How are teachers collaborating with students about their learning?

4. Discuss the importance of student learning communities in your school.

5. How do teachers form relationships with students at your school?

Transform Academy Session 8 Activities

ACTIVITY 6.1 HONING OUR CRAFT

Intended Outcome: To provide an opportunity for participants to reflect, discuss, and develop a plan of action resulting in students' perceptions of engagement in the classroom

Preparation: Arrange the training area so there are areas for small groups to sit comfortably while completing the group activities. Chart paper and markers should be available for each group.

Please visit http://resources.corwin.com/MindingTheFuture to access the online resources for this book.

Facilitation:

1. The facilitator opens the session with a brief review of the four essential questions they were accustomed to responding to in their PLCs:

   - What is it we want our students to learn?

   - How will we know if our students are learning?

   - How will we respond when students do not learn?

   - How can we extend and enrich the learning for students who have demonstrated proficiency?

2. The facilitator groups participants and directs them to work as table groups to create a compare and contrast graphic organizer. Using the Four Essential Questions they respond to in their PLCs and Practices to Support Student Engagement as the two areas of focus, each group works to determine the differences and similarities between the two areas. As the group members share ideas, one person writes the information on the graphic organizer. (If you prefer, use the partially completed example in Online Resource Y.1 and ask participants to complete the similarities section of the graphic organizer.)

3. Each group shares the ideas recorded on their graphic organizer. The facilitator should encourage the participants to comment as each group shares the information.

4. Next the facilitator directs the participants to work in their groups to consider the following questions:

   a. Looking at both areas of focus, who is typically in control of the information and actions in that area? Why is that so?

   b. How might you go about learning the students' thoughts and ideas related to student engagement?

   c. How might your personal learning plan address these issues?

   As each group responds to the questions, the information should be added to the graphic organizer.

5. Each group hangs the graphic organizer on the wall and shares their responses to the questions with the whole group. Once again, the facilitator should encourage the participants to comment as each group shares the information.

6. Working in campus groups, each campus team should outline how they intend to gain information regarding student engagement directly from the students. (The facilitator uses this information to create the spreadsheet for Step 7.)

7. Using an electronic spreadsheet that all participants can access, each campus team should respond to the required sections of the chart. (Online Resource Y.2 provides a sample spreadsheet and results from Step 6.)

8. The facilitator uses the results on the spreadsheet to group teachers according to common areas of interest. The groups begin creating the necessary documents for completing the particular area of interest (e.g., surveys, questions for 1:1 meetings, student panels with teachers, student panels with the principal, and shadowing of students).

9. Once the documents are completed, each group files them in the group electronic file storage system (e.g., Google Drive, Dropbox).

Suggested Action Items

Action Items	Progress Checks			
1. Review steps taken from the last chapter. Make planning adjustments and communication updates as needed.	☐ Not started	☐ In progress	☐ Completed	☐ NA
2. Prioritize your needs and complete the professional learning activities in this chapter.				
• Activity 6.1 Honing Our Craft	☐ Not started	☐ In progress	☐ Completed	☐ NA
3. Form a team and complete the following tasks:				
• Check for any local policies and procedures regarding the use of student surveys	☐ Not started	☐ In progress	☐ Completed	☐ NA
• Check for any local policies and procedures regarding shadowing or observing students	☐ Not started	☐ In progress	☐ Completed	☐ NA
• Consider whether additional training is needed for writing survey questions, observation statements, and ensuring confidentiality of student data	☐ Not started	☐ In progress	☐ Completed	☐ NA
4. Continue to schedule time to assist teachers with personal learning plans.	☐ Not started	☐ In progress	☐ Completed	☐ NA
5. Review calendars for study, meeting, journaling, data checks, and communicating results.	☐ Not started	☐ In progress	☐ Completed	☐ NA

CHAPTER 7

Sustaining the Momentum

Session 9

If you are working on something exciting that you really care about, you don't have to be pushed. The vision pulls you.

—STEVE JOBS

Getting Acquainted With This Chapter

Definition of the Learning Fair: the culmination of months of professional collaboration resulting in success stories and an opportunity for the Transform Academy participants to show their experiential growth. The Learning Fair thus inspired annual continuation of a successful professional learning process! Visitors were able to hear from the practitioners who flourished while their students led the learning. This chapter highlights the way inspiration resulted from practitioners sharing with each other to sustain the momentum of innovation in the learning environment.

Welcome to the Learning Fair

A year of work, learning, dreaming, researching, reflection, growth, collaborating, planning, risk taking, and innovation came to an end. And there is amazing news to share! As a result, students are increasingly engaged in transformed learning environments while the teachers were minding the future in a professional setting in which their voice leads the way. It is time for the Learning Fair!

The Learning Fair is a key action step in the academy's project design. It provides a place and time for participants to review their groundbreaking learning and state of the art work. Walking into a Transform Academy Learning Fair can only be described as a school district's version of a red-carpet affair, complete with lights, action, and, of course, lots of cameras and social media.

As the teachers prepared their areas the morning of the Learning Fair, it was evident they wanted to know what other academy teachers had accomplished as a result of their involvement in the academy. They visited with one another, viewing artifacts and asking questions in search of more information to drive changes in their own classrooms. Not only did this prepare them for the actual Learning Fair, but it also gave them an opportunity to observe their colleagues' presentation styles. This would be important for them because they would be leading the learning at their own campuses the following year.

This practice presentation also helped to prepare them for the wide range of visitors expected to attend the Learning Fair. By now they were familiar with central office personnel and the superintendent because many of them had attended at least one session during the year. However, they were not familiar with many of the school board members and community members who were also invited to stop by to learn from teachers who were eager to share their innovations. Arriving guests were greeted in the foyer outside the exhibit hall with video coverage of the year's events, school and district branding banners, informative sign-in tables, and welcoming school mascots. The teachers assumed their roles as leaders of learning as they skillfully presented and shared the changes that took place in their classrooms during the year. Standing beside their principals, the teachers shared their learning experiences and how their instruction and student engagement had been impacted by their involvement in the Transform Academy. This was a culminating opportunity to share the learning experiences that would keep the momentum moving forward for a new cohort the next year.

On Learning Fair day, the projects presented are as varied as our learners. Displays include new ways to incorporate technology, classroom redesigns, curriculum realignments, and instructional methods. See Figure 7.1 for the example categories of the displays.

Figure 7.1 Learning Fair Display Examples

Display Category	Examples
Technology	• Virtual learning • Blogging • Online learning platforms such as Google Classroom • Online libraries • Online portfolios • Online notebooks • Student-built websites • Coding • Scientific tools for measuring and calculating outcomes
Classroom Designs	• Teacher designed and built furniture • Purchased furniture • Furniture with integrated technology • High top tables • Modular seating • Flexible technology arrangements • Rugs • Counters with adjustable stools • Color and texture choices • Collaborative learning spaces • Quiet/introspective learning spaces
Curriculum and Instruction	• Assessment for learning • Personalized learning paths • Videos by learning standard built by teachers and students • Standards-based grading • Visible learning • Project-based learning

After a stimulating morning of sharing and motivating, our teachers moved to a beautiful post–Learning Fair luncheon sponsored by grateful parents. During this time, they relaxed with their principals and reflected on the year. Summer was coming and they were ready. Many would be presenting at training sessions for fellow teachers;

others were off to conferences or would be working on innovation teams to continue the momentum started by the Transform Academy in other classrooms throughout the district. Following lunch, one last task remained. We asked the teachers to complete a last benchmark on the district's strategic plan: a participant survey. This survey provides answers to the questions, "Should we continue the Transform Academy, and if so, what should we maintain or improve?" The processing of the results from this survey is described later in this chapter. The data gained from the participant survey would guide the future professional learning involved in the next Transform Academy.

Multi-Year Planning Cycle

As with any cycle of learning, the end of the academy year leads us to think about the upcoming academic year and the new Transform Academy to come. As facilitators, we took what we learned from the year-long experience of working with teachers toward their future-ready goals and the insights they shared with us along the way, and we used those data to inform the planning of the next Transform Academy. All successful endeavors begin with an informed, solid plan.

Our academy involved three planning levels aligned together in a continuous multi-year cycle (see Figure 7.2). First the Academy facilitators wrote the district's plan for the academy. This plan outlined the goals, performance measures, and action steps to develop professional learning led by teacher voice. It was part of the overall district plan and was intentionally flexible so that as we grew changes could be made. This plan guided the project design for the academy sessions based

Figure 7.2 **Transform Academy Planning and Alignment Cycle**

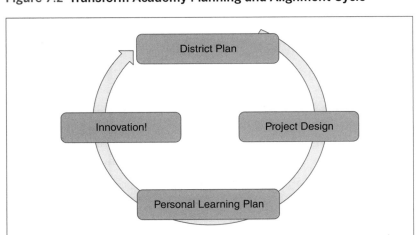

on Project Based Learning (PBL; see Figure I.1 Sample Project Based Learning Design: Transform Academy). Then as part of the project design, teachers wrote individual or group personal learning plans, as described in Chapter 4. From the personal learning plans came exciting and replicable innovative strategies displayed in the Learning Fair. Thus, the aligned planning cycle continued to the next year!

As we worked in this cycle, we gained insights about the planning steps needed to sustain our academy project. To begin, our initial district plan was collaboratively developed and piloted with a small group (one school to start) to test the processes. The pilot was then expanded into a three-year timeline with additional teachers added each time. As you may expect, the action steps of this first plan were broad, and the pilot group of teachers assisted in writing the more specific implementation steps for the years to follow. The experiences and suggestions shared by teacher-participants revealed that there would always be planning additions and deletions throughout the life of the academy. Planning sessions were held after each Transform Academy. During these meetings key district personnel, principals, teacher participants, and the facilitation team focused on end of the year survey data and Learning Fair presentations, in order to improve future academy experiences and operationalize exemplary classroom innovations on a wider basis in the district. For example, as furniture and equipment was replaced in older buildings or purchased for new ones, a much-needed catalog of academy-inspired selections became available. Choices included tables of varying shapes, colors, and sizes; soft, flexible seating; digital devices for classroom and home use; and charging stations for electronics. The group's willingness to collaborate with us provided a critical element—a professional learning and innovation process led by the real experts, our teachers!

The Significance of the Learning Fair

Enthusiasm for sustaining the Transform Academy built each year as teachers presented their innovations to other professionals and the community. Although the Learning Fair was the last session of the year with the entire academy, planning for a project of this scale began prior to the first session of the year. The facilitation team, along with a core group of teachers, developed a monthly planning guide to monitor the progress of the participants' activities toward the end of the year showcase of experiences (see Online Resource Z). This guide was informed by the activities in the monthly sessions as well as their personal learning plans and information gathered by the teacher participants. For example, they would send pictures of changes in their classrooms, social media posts about thoughts and ideas related to innovation in education, and allow academy facilitators to video them in their classrooms. The personal learning plans they developed, revisited, and revised throughout the year provided a framework for their presentation as well as a means of sharing the impact and outcomes of their work. Their work also would contribute to their future campus plans and the momentum of the next Transform Academy. These proactive planning process allowed the teachers to build their portfolios for display at the Learning Fair.

During the afternoon of the day of the Learning Fair, the teachers and principals were ready to reflect on the Transform Academy experience. An online survey was provided for each teacher to complete independently (see Online Resource AA.1). The purpose of the survey was twofold: to provide the teachers with a forum for reflecting on their personal learning from this year as well as their next steps, and to provide the facilitators with feedback that would be used as we began developing the plan for the next cohort of Transform Academy. The survey yielded a variety of responses (see Figure 7.3).

Figure 7.3 End of Year Survey Responses From Participant Teachers

1. List three big ideas you learned from your participation in the Transform Academy sessions this year.

- Change is good.
- Fear of the unknown is to be expected.
- Opportunities need to be provided for students to take control of their learning.
- Students need choice in their learning.
- Integrating apps in instruction should be purposeful.
- Social media can be a learning tool.
- The visioning document is a tool that supports transformation.
- Maker spaces provide opportunities for developing critical thinking skills.
- Project-based learning supports student choice in learning.
- Blended learning can support students in the learning process.
- Patience while learning new tools is critical.
- Staying current with new technology tools leads to students being prepared for the future.

(Continued)

Figure 7.3 (Continued)

- Flexible seating and workspaces in the classroom can lead to better engagement.
- Transforming teaching and learning involves much more than technology.
- Sharing and collaborating contribute to teacher efficacy.
- A growth mindset is important for students and teachers.
- Students need to collaborate in order to be prepared for the future.
- Tests cannot be the only way we measure student learning.

2. List two ideas or practices you want to improve upon.

- Engaging in positive and impactful conversations with colleagues when they don't see the value in what I am sharing with them
- Developing student experiences that they can relate to and supports them as 21st-century learners
- Students collaborating in a variety of content areas
- Providing more opportunities for hands-on learning integrated with PBL
- Publicizing and sharing the transformations in my classroom
- Online student data tracking
- Integrating technology in an authentic and seamless manner
- Managing 1:1 technology implementation more efficiently
- Planning for instruction in a more meaningful way
- Coding club
- Expanding PBL in a 1:1 environment
- Providing opportunities for students to learn from one another
- Extending student collaboration to involve students in other classrooms
- Creating videos to use in a blended learning environment
- Providing more opportunities for flipped learning
- Developing and utilizing choice boards with students
- Engaging students in goal setting and providing effective feedback

3. List one idea you plan to explore next year.

- Technology tools for the ELA classroom
- Google trainer certification
- Assessments aligned to the premises in the visioning document
- Project-based learning
- Implementation of maker spaces

- Coding and robotics
- Websites to facilitate instruction in all content areas
- Digital portfolios
- Flipped or faux-flipped classrooms
- Visible learning
- Technology badges for teachers

4. What shifts have you made in the learning environment, student engagement, and instructional practices as a result of your participation in Transform Academy?

- Improved mobility in the classroom
- Improved technology integration in instruction in all content areas
- Developed flexible seating practices that supported instruction and student engagement needs
- Incorporated more hands-on practices in the classroom
- Improved use of laptops as an instructional tool
- Demonstrated for my students that teachers are lifelong learners
- Allowed students to be involved in the teaching and learning process
- Improved practices related to self-efficacy (teacher and students)
- Increased comfort with risk taking
- Offer students more choices and ways to demonstrate understanding of concepts
- Empowered students to use technology as a tool for collaboration and creativity
- Empowered to look for innovative ways for students to demonstrate learning
- Recaptured my passion for teaching
- Found my LOVE for teaching again
- Transformed my mindset
- Provide time for students to explore topics that are relevant to them
- Personalize learning for my students

5. How have you shared your learning at your campus this year?

- Grade-level training during PLCs
- Mini-presentations at faculty meetings
- Invited colleagues into my classroom to see the students in action
- Updates throughout the year at Leadership Team meetings
- Panel discussion on campus

Once the teachers reviewed the results of the survey, we began looking ahead to next year. Our final activity involved revisiting their learning from the year and developing possible topics for discussion and professional learning at their campuses (see Activity 7.1 Leading a Future-Ready Vision in this chapter). The intent was to provide an opportunity for the participants to reflect on the learning from the year and to initiate a long-term professional development plan based on their experiences in the Transform Academy. The teachers participated in a collaborative mind mapping activity to discuss the results of the survey and to prioritize the needs for future academies. In addition, they debated the strengths, weaknesses, opportunities, and challenges (SWOC) of the series of academy sessions. This review filled with teacher voice would guide the sessions for the next cohort of academy participants.

The day would not be complete without acknowledging each Transform Academy teacher with a certificate for the willingness to forge ahead into the unknown and maintain a relentless focus on preparing students to be future ready. They were honored to be a part of this group of teachers and confident that, with the support of their principals, they could lead their colleagues on their own campuses through a process similar to the one they experienced this year. The Transform Academy certificate not only represented their active engagement in a professional development model that allowed them to lead their own learning but it signified a new beginning, a transformation of sorts. It was now their responsibility *and honor* to challenge and lead their colleagues through transforming and minding the future.

KEY IDEAS

In this chapter, we describe how teachers displayed their innovative learning environments at the Session 9 Learning Fair. This successful exhibition inspired a multi-year plan to continue the professional learning in the Transform Academy. The display of innovation at the Learning Fair by trailblazing teachers sustained the momentum of innovation for the future.

1. How does your campus share the results of innovation?

2. What process do you have in place when outcomes are not optimal?

3. Why is it important to have a long-range plan?

4. Why is it necessary to have individual and collaborative reflection?

5. How does your campus celebrate success in learning?

Transform Academy Session 9 Activities

ACTIVITY 7.1 LEADING A FUTURE-READY VISION

Intended Outcome: To provide an opportunity for the teachers to reflect on the learning from the year and to focus on a long-term professional development plan based on their experiences in the Transform Academy

Preparation: Prior to opening the discussion, the facilitator should review the results of the survey completed earlier in the day, particularly the first question focused on things they learned through their participation in the academy this year. These ideas will be used to create a mind map the group will complete.

Facilitation:

1. The facilitator opens the discussion with a review of the ideas and concepts participants responded to in Item 1 of the survey. (See Online Resource AA.1 for survey statements and questions.) The facilitator then displays a partial mind map. (The mind map was created by placing the ideas from the survey into categories and labeling the categories. Figure 7.4 is an example of a partial mind map that includes the big ideas gathered from the survey.)

Please visit http://resources.corwin.com/MindingTheFuture to access the online resources for this book.

online resources

Figure 7.4 Sample Mind Map of Big Ideas

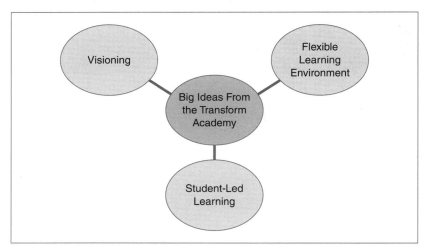

2. The facilitator divides the large group into three smaller groups. Each group is assigned one of the big ideas on the chart. The group moves to an assigned area of the room to further develop the mind map.

3. On a piece of chart paper, each group begins identifying the key understandings of the particular idea assigned. (Figure 7.5 is an example of the key understandings related to the big ideas.)

4. Once each group has completed the assigned section of the chart, the facilitator rotates the groups to the next chart. The facilitator directs the groups to read the information on the chart. If new ideas are suggested, they add the new information to the chart.

5. The facilitator rotates the groups a final time and directs the groups to read the information on the chart. Once again, if new ideas are suggested they add the information to the chart.

6. The groups complete a final review of the three charts before returning to their tables.

7. The facilitator directs the participants to work in campus groups to prioritize the big ideas into a sequence of implementation specific to their campuses.

8. The facilitator leads a discussion using the following questions to prompt conversation:

   • How might you use this information to develop a plan for continuing the momentum at your campus next year?

   • What might this form of collaborative professional learning look like at your campus?

   • How will you ensure teacher and student voice is included in the development of the professional learning plan?

Figure 7.5 Sample Mind Map of Big Ideas With Responses

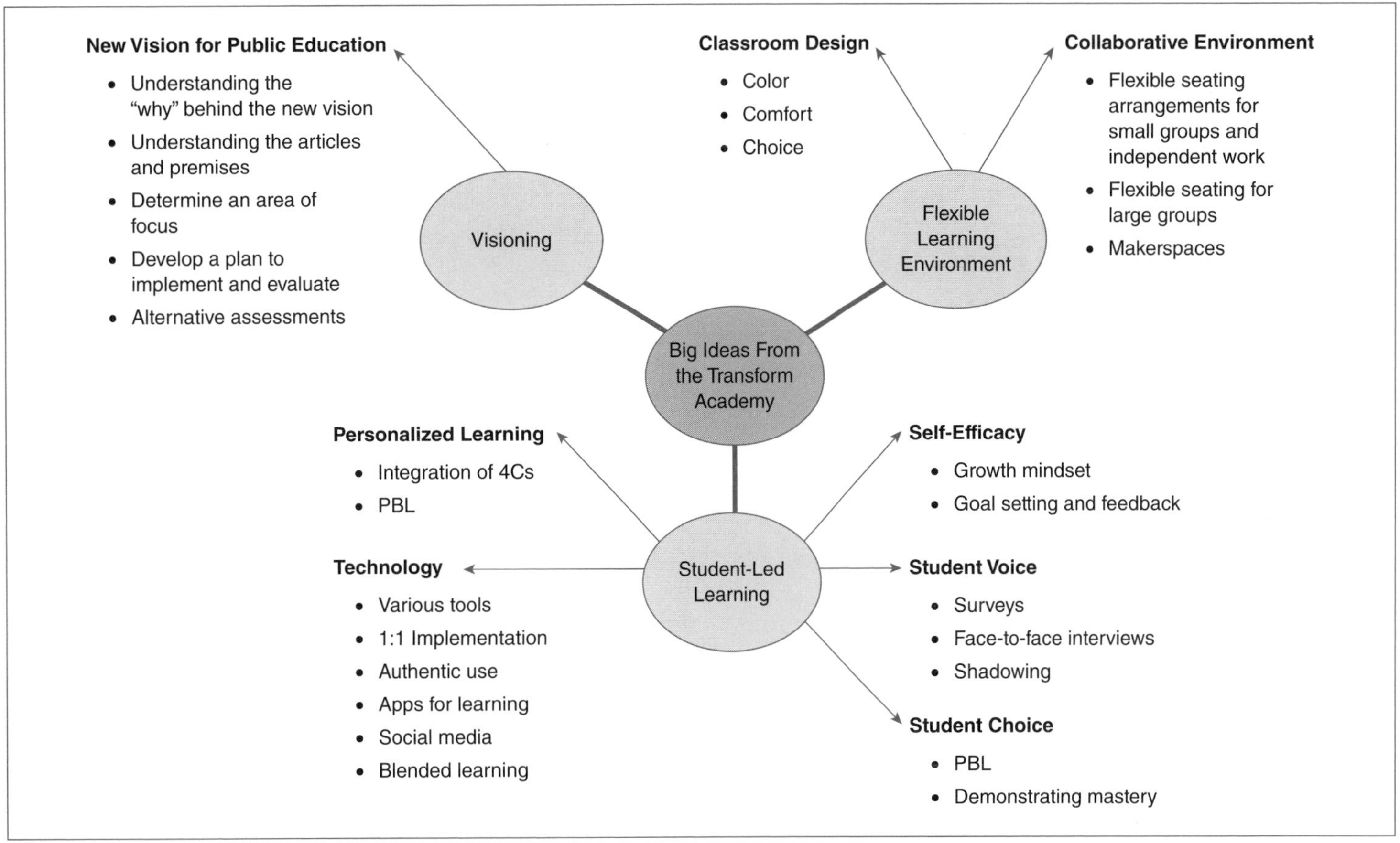

New Vision for Public Education

- Understanding the "why" behind the new vision
- Understanding the articles and premises
- Determine an area of focus
- Develop a plan to implement and evaluate
- Alternative assessments

Classroom Design

- Color
- Comfort
- Choice

Collaborative Environment

- Flexible seating arrangements for small groups and independent work
- Flexible seating for large groups
- Makerspaces

Visioning

Big Ideas From the Transform Academy

Flexible Learning Environment

Student-Led Learning

Personalized Learning

- Integration of 4Cs
- PBL

Technology

- Various tools
- 1:1 Implementation
- Authentic use
- Apps for learning
- Social media
- Blended learning

Self-Efficacy

- Growth mindset
- Goal setting and feedback

Student Voice

- Surveys
- Face-to-face interviews
- Shadowing

Student Choice

- PBL
- Demonstrating mastery

9. The facilitator reminds the participants to reflect on the three questions and their responses as they complete a SWOC Analysis (Strengths, Weaknesses, Opportunities, and Challenges) for the number 1 priority on the list. The campus team completes each area on the template. (See Online Resource AA.2 for the SWOC analysis template.)

10. The facilitator pulls the group together and provides an opportunity for the campus teams to share their responses on the SWOC template. As teams share participants are encouraged to make revisions to their SWOC analysis as needed.

11. Each campus team develops a plan for sharing the priorities and SWOC analysis with the campus principal prior to beginning their work on the Campus Improvement Plan.

Suggested Action Items

Action Items	Progress Checks			
1. Review steps taken from the last chapter. Make planning adjustments and communication updates as needed.	☐ Not started	☐ In progress	☐ Completed	☐ NA
2. Prioritize your needs and complete the professional learning activities in this chapter.				
a. Activity 7.1 Leading a Future Ready Vision	☐ Not started	☐ In progress	☐ Completed	☐ NA
3. Review calendars for study, meeting, journaling, data checks, and communicating results.	☐ Not started	☐ In progress	☐ Completed	☐ NA

CHAPTER 8

Parting Thoughts

> The only way to do great work is to love what you do. If you haven't found it yet, keep looking. Don't settle.
>
> —STEVE JOBS

Open Doors and Minds

To begin our final chapter, imagine these scenarios at your school . . .

A curious child peers into a Transform Academy teacher's classroom. As he carefully looks around, it is apparent he is contrasting his own class with this one. He sees colorful carpets, tables you can write on, beanbag chairs, and digital devices. The students are sitting in groups or standing around an electronic whiteboard. They look very busy, and surprisingly, they keep talking as they work. Sometimes one student reaches over and clicks on another student's tablet. "Wow!" he thinks. Finally, he finds the teacher who seems almost hidden, compared to his class where the teacher is usually sitting in one of two places. The Transform Academy teacher is perched on a yoga ball listening to a group of students share their ideas. When the teacher motions him in, our curious student says, "I saw the plaque on your door. What's a Transform Academy? Why does this room look different? Where are the worksheets and the folders to cover your work? Why does everyone get to talk? Why are you sitting on that funny stool asking kids what they want to learn about today?"

In another school, two students walk by a classroom between class periods. They glance into the room and nudge each other. "I want to be in that class next year. Look at the high-top tables and those great stools. They get to work in groups and listen to music. What a way to learn math! My friend is in that class, and he says that they help the younger kids at another school with problem solving once a week. They use their computers to communicate with them. Look over there at the live video feed set up in the corner. Today they are going to use it for a virtual field trip. They are visiting a design studio to learn about how geometry is used to build new workspaces. Sure looks like fun! Interesting plaque by the door, too. Says he is some kind of transformer teacher. Cool!"

A Professional Learning Community meeting begins with jovial voices ready to discuss the results from their latest project-based learning plan. As they gather around a conference table, each teacher holds an electronic device opened to the group's online student data and planning tools. Although the type of device they use varies, their focus does not. They begin their meeting with an eye on student engagement. The discussion starts with a comparison of the project's learning outcomes and the results from a student survey. The student responses give them some clarity about what they need to keep for the next project, but they are unsure about deleting a couple of ideas, so they decide to conduct a focus group to determine next steps. As the meeting draws to a close, the team checks their calendars to make sure everyone is ready for their day to shadow a student. One teacher says, "I learn so much every time we do this. It helps me understand all the things my kids juggle in school and how we can make learning relevant to their needs now and in the future. Plus, I love eating extra cheese pizza in the cafeteria!"

Building Your Transform Academy

As you develop plans for your academy, you will find three elements ultimately lead to success: the project facilitators, the participants, and your definition of professional learning. Here we offer some closing ideas from our own professional learning.

Role of the Lead Facilitator

The Transform Academy facilitator is a project manager, planning coordinator, event organizer, and most important, a benevolent guardian. This person is the pivotal connection between the teachers, their visions, and possibilities. Using a collaborative planning cycle allows the facilitator to design and monitor the project, make adjustments as needed, and document innovative results. A Transform Academy facilitator is a lifelong learner whose own collaborative innovator mindset is strengthened by a "whatever it takes" attitude. She values consensus in professional learning topics and sees herself as a guide and not the "expert."

As the facilitator works through an academy year, she is aware that it will not be without obstacles and possibly conflict, but she knows that building trust and blocking blame will allow risk taking to continue. Trusting relationships in the academy occur between the participants and with the facilitator. Participants should feel that suggestions are always valued; questions will be answered; promises will be upheld; and support is ever-present. In a word, a facilitator "listens." She listens to teachers, research, students, community, and district departments, then acts with grace and precision in the best interest of students. So, remember the facilitator will need support when traveling this road. She will also need space for her own learning and a support team for ideas, reinforcement, and "leg work." A Transform Academy facilitator does not see locks on doors because she believes there is always a key hidden somewhere in the collective wisdom of the academy participants.

Know Your Participants

We will always be grateful to our Transform Academy teachers and their principals for stepping into minding the future with willing hearts and positive attitudes. Their work has inspired and energized other educators and engaged students as influential learners. As you review the list of participants for your academy, we offer this thinking.

- Look for **isolated innovators.** They are waiting for a chance to share in a risk-free environment. Be ready to encourage them to collaborate. They may also need models to show them how to work in a team.

- Look for the **status quo collaborators**. They could be the team who will move forward quickly if they feel collectively empowered and supported. They will worry about the consequences of their risks, so have frequent contact with them.

- Be ready to encourage the **isolated status quo** during the professional development sessions. As they see the work of their peers they, too, may start to innovate. They need to see and feel success. A nudge from trusted peers may help.

- Be grateful for the **collaborative innovators** but also be prepared! They have energy to spare. Be ready to run with them as they create transformational learning environments and practices. Research, planning, goal setting, monitoring, and journaling will be key to showcasing and sustaining their work.

Professional Learning Defined

Your definition of professional learning will also define your academy. As we designed our academy, we knew that growing in an educator's craft involves consistent opportunities to learn. Inspirational, transformative professional learning comes about in many ways. When we engage in regular collaborative opportunities where instructional ideas are intertwined with research and data, an educator's practice is improved exponentially and students benefit from new learning experiences. Our professional discussions almost always involve learning something new, and this new learning is professional learning. When a different instructional method is implemented in the classroom and time is given to reflect about and refine the outcome with fellow teachers, we have professional learning. When a learning community reads a book, examines the research, and then decides to try a new strategy, they have professional learning. Attendance at a conference or visits to future-ready businesses to study how to increase student engagement is professional learning!

Quality professional learning opens our minds to breakthrough thinking and says to fellow educators that professional learning is ongoing, constant, and necessary for improvement. Through supportive team endeavors teacher isolation decreases, collaboration increases, status quo thinking diminishes, and innovation transforms the learning culture. Teachers with a passion for learning will inspire other teachers and their students to grow and learn (Hattie, 2012).

Finally, professional learning in a Transform Academy is not about what we already know. Nor is the academy a place where teachers are told what they need to know. It is not a series of meetings about core content standards or conduct rules. It is a place where teachers do what they do best: lead their own learning while minding our future treasures—students. So, listen to teacher voice, be open to dreaming, and encourage innovation. The journey itself is professional learning!

References

Combs, J. P., Edmonson, S., & Harris, S. (2013). *The trust factor: Strategies for school leaders.* New York, NY: Eye on Education.

Couros, G. (2015). *Innovator mindset.* San Diego, CA: Burgess Consulting.

DuFour, R., DuFour, R., Eaker, R., & Many, T. (2006). *Learning by doing: A handbook for professional learning communities at work.* Bloomington, IN: Solution Tree Press.

Dweck, C. (2006). *Mindset: The new psychology of success.* New York, NY: Ballantine.

Einstein, A. (2013). *The ultimate quotable Einstein.* Princeton, NJ: Princeton University Press.

Hattie, J. (2012). *Visible learning for teachers: Maximizing impact on learning.* Thousand Oaks, CA: Corwin.

Learning Forward. (2017). *Standards for professional learning.* Retrieved from https://learningforward.org/standards-for-professional-learning

Marzano, R., Heflebower, T., Hoegh, J., Warrick, P., & Grift, G. (2016). *Collaborative teams that transform schools.* Bloomington, IN: Marzano Research.

Milton, P. (2015). *Shifting minds 3.0: Redefining the learning landscape in Canada.* Toronto, ON: C21 Canada.

Moore, W. Retrieved from https://www.youtube.com/watch?v=oFMDEE6_51w

National Education Association. (2015). *Preparing 21st century students for a global society: An educator's guide to the four C's.* Washington, DC: Author.

National School Reform Faculty Harmony Education Center. (2017, November 9). *Protocols.* Retrieved from https://www.nsrfharmony.org

November, A. (2012). *Who owns the learning? Preparing students for success in the digital age.* Bloomington, IN: Solution Tree Press.

Partnership for 21st Century Learning. (2015). *Framework for 21st century learning.* Washington, DC: Author.

Texas Association of School Administrators. (2008). *Creating a new vision for public education in Texas.* Austin: Texas Leadership Center.

Walsh, J. A., & Sattes, B. D. (2011). *Thinking through quality questioning: Deepening student engagement.* Thousand Oaks, CA: Corwin.

Wujec, T. (2017). *Marshmallow challenge.* Retrieved from https://www.tomwujec.com/design-projects/marshmallow-challenge/

Index

CORWIN

A SAGE Publishing Company

CORWIN HAS ONE MISSION: to enhance education through intentional professional learning.

We build long-term relationships with our authors, educators, clients, and associations who partner with us to develop and continuously improve the best evidence-based practices that establish and support lifelong learning.

THE PROFESSIONAL LEARNING ASSOCIATION

Learning Forward is a nonprofit, international membership association of learning educators committed to one vision in K–12 education: Excellent teaching and learning every day. To realize that vision, Learning Forward pursues its mission to build the capacity of leaders to establish and sustain highly effective professional learning. Information about membership, services, and products is available from www.learningforward.org.

Solutions you want. Experts you trust. Results you need.